How Girls Achieve

How Girls Achieve

SALLY A. NUAMAH

Harvard University Press

Cambridge, Massachusetts

London, England

2019

Library of Congress Cataloging-in-Publication Data
is available from loc.gov
ISBN 978-0-674-98022-8 (alk. paper)

For Afua Serwaah

Contents

Preface

School is her refuge.
ref · uge
noun
A condition of being safe or sheltered
from pursuit, danger, or trouble.

AN OLDER WOMAN spoke to me with clear eyes and a calm tone, slowly and deliberately so that I might imagine her and Ghana in the 1970s:

> I didn't grow up with my mom because my mom was young when she had me. When my father died, my mother was learning hairdressing, so she moved . . . She was hustling, so she wouldn't have to live with *her* mother.
>
> She had the other two that came after me [when] she was still young, around 22 or 23, so my grandmother raised me. I loved my grandmother raising me. She gave me a lot of wisdom. The only thing though is, no matter how poor or what condition, you will still miss your mother. There are certain things that make me unsure or that affect me still today because of my mother.
>
> Although my grandma loved me, I felt like I didn't belong. I felt like the rest had some type of freedom that

I didn't have. I felt like I had to conform, that I had to listen. I felt like I could not say no when they did because I didn't have that kind of entitlement.

When school opened, I would have to wait until everyone else got their school supplies before someone will notice that I didn't have mine.

[Being motherless] always pushed me a little to the back. It made me a quiet person, and as a result, school became my refuge. I loved going to school.

There, I could express myself. I could show people I was better.

That is *my* mother's story.

She was born and raised in Ghana, the daughter of teenage parents, although her father died soon after her birth.

My mother used school as a refuge from her home life.

She went to one of Ghana's best secondary schools, St. Monica's, and later entered secretarial trade school. Soon after, she was admitted into the University of Cape Coast but was unable to afford the tuition.

My mother's educational journey came to an end.

She met my father at twenty-eight, they married, and she decided to migrate with him to America in search of better opportunities. Following their arrival, my brother and I were born, but by the time I was five my mother and father divorced.

My mother raised my brother and me.

She worked as a hotel maid and then as a parking lot patroller in Chicago throughout our childhood, adolescence, and young adulthood. In her twenty-six years of working in America, she never earned more than eleven dollars an hour.

My father was present sporadically.

I am the child of immigrant parents, a first-generation American. I was raised by a single mother on a small salary in a low-income neighborhood in Chicago. I am a woman, and I am Black.

I fit most of the statistical categorizations of disadvantage.

In fact, by most statistical models, it is unlikely that I would have gained the education and prestige necessary to catalog my mother's experiences in a published book. Yet my mother's educational aspirations have survived through me.

School has been my refuge.

Inspired by my mother's example, for the past ten years I have collected data on the educational experiences and aspirations of girls in South Africa, the United States, and Ghana. This book represents my attempt to develop a cohesive message from these data.

If this book has resonance in the world, I hope it leaves people with something like the following:

May the schoolhouse be a refuge for all girls . . . like it was for me and my mother.

How Girls Achieve

Introduction

LETTING GIRLS LEARN

> When I was young, I thought that a life of equality,
> wisdom and justice would be my birthright if only
> I worked hard at school . . . I was wrong.
>
> —HOPE CHIGUDU

I AM GOING TO START THIS BOOK where most people end. I conclude that to let girls learn, schools must first protect them. Then, they must teach them three skills: confidence, strategy, and transgression. Finally, and perhaps most important, they must reimagine what it means to achieve.

Allow me to explain.

I begin with the premise that no one selects the circumstances of their birth, yet one's circumstances directly affect one's life chances. Children born poor, female, a person of color, differently abled, or LGBTQ+, for example, suffer disruptions to the length and quality of their lives. And that is unfair.

Because it is unfair—and a central tenet of liberal democracies is nondiscrimination—if we claim to value fairness, we must intervene. To be clear, we must ensure that the circumstances of one's birth do not dictate the remainder of one's life.

The question is, How?

I argue that no institution or social system is more likely to improve the life trajectory of the disadvantaged than schools. Not voting. Not infrastructure. Not employment. Schools.

John Dewey noted, "the moral responsibility of the school, and of those who conduct it, is to society. The school is fundamentally an institution erected by society to do a certain specific work,—to exercise a certain specific function in *maintaining* the life and *advancing* the welfare of society."[1] It is unsurprising, then, that past systems of education were used by countries to maintain inequality—take Jim Crow segregation in the United States or Bantu Education in South Africa. Conversely, systems of education have been used by countries to repair past injustices and advance equality—take school desegregation, beginning with the 1954 *Brown v. Board of Education* decision in the United States and the provisional constitution of South Africa in 1994.

In modern liberal democracies, schools are tasked with providing all students with the tools they need to achieve (as a mechanism for becoming productive workers and good citizens). To do this, schools focus on improving the "quality" of schools, measured by the cognitive development of students or the instructional skills of teachers. These improvements are aimed at reforming school leadership, approaches to teaching, and classroom structure.

However, as schools work to become higher quality institutions, they often fail to provide certain groups, the largest of which is girls, with an educational environment that protects them. Nor do they imbue them with the confidence to believe in themselves, the strategies they need to navigate barriers, nor the audacity to transgress societal norms. In fact, most schools are completely unprepared to educate girls in an equitable fashion, if *equitable* is defined as girls receiving what they need to succeed. I offer the story of Ezra and Jude as an illustration.

Ezra and Jude attend public school in a large city. Yet while Ezra attends school the full twenty-three days in each month, Jude only attends school eighteen days in each month. What explains the difference in school attendance between Ezra and Jude? And does it matter if they are both high academic achievers?

Ezra attends a school that anticipates and alleviates potential gendered challenges, like the fact that sanitary pads are expensive and thus being able to afford them can impact her ability to attend school during her menstrual cycle.[2] Accordingly, Ezra's school offers its students sanitary pads at no cost and as needed.

Jude, on the other hand, attends a school that does not address the gender inequities she might face. The school, like most across the globe, does not provide complimentary sanitary pads to its students. Additionally, the school hasn't had flush toilets since it was constructed. In fact, only 60 percent of the schools in Jude's city have flush toilets at all.

Although many do not realize the effect a lack of access to these basic resources may have, such a lack has a major impact on Jude's education. Jude cannot attend school during her menstrual cycle—up to six of every twenty-three days.

The difference between Ezra and Jude does not represent a dichotomy between the West and the Global South. It does not represent disparate countries, but disparate times. In developed and developing economies, Jude is our present, but hopefully Ezra might be our future.

The current reality is that a growing population of girls across the globe attend schools that never had them in mind to begin with. Schools that are assumed safe but give them their first experiences with sexual abuse and rape at the hands of male peers and teachers. Schools that are assumed accepting but bully and suspend girls for not meeting traditional conceptions of femininity. Schools that are assumed habitable but lack basic sanitary needs, including flush toilets, toilet paper, and sanitary pads.

The schools that overlook gender inequities are not exceptional or unique. They are the default. This means that even an academically rigorous school can be an inequitable one.

At the very least, Jude, like Ezra, is enrolled in school. Globally, over 130 million girls—more than twice the total population of students in the entire United States—are not in school at all.[3] This is a tragic waste in part because educating girls is associated with a plethora of positive outcomes: Educated women raise healthier children, are more likely to become economically independent, and are more likely contribute to social and economic development.

Fortunately, over the past two decades we have seen the emergence of widespread global initiatives (for example, Girl Rising and #62MillionGirls in support of the Let Girls Learn initiative) that are designed to increase the number of girls in school. Unfortunately, despite these initiatives, most schools do not address the educational experiences of the girls who *can* get educational access: the experiences of girls like Jude, who struggles to achieve at an institution that values her good grades but discounts or disregards the gender inequities that keep her from attending school consistently.[4]

Today, many schools across the globe reproduce and perpetuate gender inequities. They are hostile toward girls and women. Still, many of us who care about gender, identify as feminist, or show up at women's rallies overlook the ways in which schools fail to practice the equity we preach, so long as they are "quality" schools where students "achieve." This needs to change.

What It Means to Achieve

Current measures of achievement fail to capture the educational experiences of the whole student. Instead, achievement is typically defined by students' academic performance. Education literature describes a link between academic achievement and the level of parents' education or economic status. It is theorized that parental resources enable children to have the insights, access, and assistance necessary to do well in school. Thus, differences in social and economic background are often used to explain educational disparities in academic achievement within the classroom.

A growing field of study on noncognitive skills demonstrates how they can contribute to academic achievement as well, even though they are traditionally left unmeasured on standardized exams. For example, noncognitive characteristics such as grit, tenacity, and self-control have been found to positively contribute to grade point average and career success.[5]

Noncognitive skills can also take the shape of an academic mindset. There is perhaps no academic mindset more well known than the growth mindset, one half of a concept developed by Carol Dweck. The growth mindset theorizes that students who do well in school typically have an attitude of potential success (for example, "I can be good at math") while others have a fixed mindset of failure ("I am not good at math"). Differences in mindsets may help explain gender gaps in academic achievement. For example, a nationally representative longitudinal study of US tenth and twelfth graders over a six-year period found that boys rate their ability to do math 27 percent higher than girls, even if they have identical math abilities.[6] This disparity is, in part, related to a finding in the same study that boys are more likely to have a growth mindset and thus view their mathematical abilities as skills which can be developed and improved. In fact, the literature on noncognitive skills suggests that the early and more widespread adoption of a growth mindset partially explains the advantage of boys over girls in the fields of science, technology, engineering, and mathematics (STEM). Girls, on the other hand, are more likely to have the noncognitive skills of self-discipline and self-regulation, which enable them to earn high grades across most other subjects.[7]

At face value, these studies of noncognitive skills appear to provide comprehensive explanations of gender disparities in achievement, but they focus too narrowly on how these skills shape performance outcomes.[8] This focus on performance outcomes contributes to an oversimplified narrative of "girls versus boys," wherein a category of high-achieving girls become evidence for individual-level success and proof that education policies are effective. Instead, studies based on noncognitive skills must account for the fact that school-aged girls have multiple negative experiences with sexual harassment, criminal justice, poverty, and racism. These experiences affect their well-being, even if they are not affecting girls' academic success.[9] In other words, educators worrying about whether their students have enough grit and adequately high test scores should be even more worried about what their students are experiencing in school and how it affects their overall well-being.

In this book I reimagine achievement not only as a measure of academic performance but also as the absence of damage from experiences with learning. In sum, to achieve is both to attain academic success and to build a healthy educational identity that allows a student to attain in different settings. I call this *net achievement*: the term *net* implies that the cost of the academic achievement is taken into account.

The Role of Schools in Improving Net Achievement for All

Schools can improve net achievement, in part, through the development of educational identities and strategic skills among their students. Like a growth mindset, these identities and skills can be unique and potentially contradictory across a population of students.[10] Most notably, studies that focus on minority students in the United States illustrate how these students must often take on multiple personal and academic identities to perform at levels similar to their majority peers.[11] One study, for instance, documents how African-American and Latinx youth in the United States form academically oriented peer groups and develop strategies for managing the multiple identities they take on at home as well as at school. The researchers attribute the development of these identities and the related management strategies to their schools' ability to enable students to "believe in their own efficacy and the power of schooling to change their lives." The researchers also note that these students "do not adopt a romantic or naïve commitment" to the ideology, thereby acknowledging that students adopt these beliefs in the context of the respective barriers they face.[12] The students' contextualized belief in themselves and the role of the school in generating this belief demonstrate how identity can be constructed by schools and used among minority youth to strategically achieve in a way that accounts for cost borne as well as benefits received.[13]

How Quality Schools Should Teach Lessons about Gender

As schools foster educational identities and strategies to manage them, they also impart (whether implicitly or explicitly) lessons about gender. Since no other institution, outside of the home, can so clearly shape the trajectory of a child's life, the way in which schools impart these lessons becomes extremely important. For example, masculinity and femininity are taught and performed through the cues sent to girls on how to be "ladies" and to boys on how to be men. When schools impart these lessons, they often do so in a way that polices gender and thus negatively contributes to students' overall educational experiences. (Examples include rules that encourage girls to cross their legs and instruct boys not to cry.) These negative educational experiences shape students' ability to effectively engage in their schools' central activities and achieve, whether academically or otherwise.

While scholars in the United States and Europe have discussed the importance of evaluating gender socialization in schools to some extent, with few exceptions these studies are typically focused on improving girls' educational access and academic performance in western settings rather than alleviating the disparate costs girls around the globe suffer for such academic performance.[14] Accordingly, efforts to improve school quality fail to create equitable experiences that produce positive educational identities for *all* girls.

A critical way to ensure that schools do not simply become reflections of inequity in the world around them—even as they seek to transform into academically superior institutions—is to create schools that take seriously the role of inequitable gender relations in their educational practices. In other words, dismantling inequitable gender relations must be included as part of an expanded approach to the ways we think about improving the quality of a school.[15] When quality schools dismantle inequitable gender relations, they ensure that the price of achievement is not dependent on an accident of birth. They prioritize net achievement and encourage students to develop their educational identities as a function of their minds and not their reproductive organs.

Eliminating Institutional Sexism

For quality schools to address inequitable gender relations properly and thus act as positive contributors to net achievement, they must take action to eliminate sexism—a system that assigns value based on sex and unfairly values one sex over the other.

Before sexism can be eliminated, it must be understood. How does sexism reveal itself in society? Camara Phyllis Jones, a physician and public health scholar, has described a three-level taxonomy of racism.[16] I adopt her approach to discuss how sexism reveals itself in society. Recognizing that systems of racism and sexism often work alongside each other, these levels are not meant to be comprehensive but rather to document some ways in which sexism constrains the ability for certain persons, in this case women and girls of color, to achieve their potential. Accordingly, based on her framework, I describe three levels of sexism:

- *Internalized sexism and self-devaluation.* The acceptance of negative messages about the limits of one's abilities based on sex, leading to behavioral shifts consistent with these negative messages. Examples include thinking, "I am not a math person and girls can't do math, so I don't want to be a mathematician." These attitudes can lead to lower levels of self-esteem and limited aspirations. They usually stem from routine interactions with negative messaging about abilities.
- *Personally mediated sexism.* Differential assumptions about the abilities, motives, and intent of others based on sex, as well as differences in action or in response. Represented by acts of commission and omission, such sexism can be unintentional and can include micro-aggressions. Examples include the failure of teachers to assign value to girls' ability to do math, which leads them to track girl students into home science courses rather than biological science courses.
- *Institutionalized sexism.* Differential or uneven access to the goods, services, and opportunities of society based on sex. This type of sexism is represented by

acts of commission, omission, and inaction in the face of need. Examples include being charged higher insurance premiums as a woman and being educated in a school without bathrooms. Institutionalized sexism denotes the way that sexism is embedded in our everyday societal practices and experiences, and the way it is perceived as normal.

Using this framework, we could try to address inequitable gender relations at school by fixing internalized sexism. We might stress "grit," "resilience," "girl power," and the need to "lean in," but this won't change the situation in which girls find themselves. Such approaches only force them to deal with it, alone. We can address personally mediated sexism by holding workshops and classes on implicit gender bias to make people aware of their assumptions in order to change their behavior, but even if people change their biased behavior, it will not change the biased institutions in which girls find themselves.[17] Thus, schools must address institutionalized sexism—unequal access to goods, services, and opportunities of society based on sex. Solving or remediating the problems associated with institutionalized sexism may diminish the impact of the other two types. So what type of school facilitates the elimination of institutional sexism?

The Elusive Promise
of Gender-Sensitive Schools

To be sure, there is already significant discussion on the importance of schools developing "girl-friendly" or "gender-responsive" environments, which are commonly defined as classrooms that are sensitive to gender-based experiences.[18] Most of these proposals emphasize the importance of acknowledging how policies and practices affect girls and boys differently and removing the barriers identified; creating opportunities to develop peer networks and friendships; encouraging women role models and using women as examples for classwork; and ensuring girls participate in the classroom and that their voices are represented as co-creators of their education.

Nonetheless, policies and practices that seek to make schools more girl-friendly often only reconstruct boundaries protecting the status quo; in other words, they allow girls to have access to education in a way that simply extends rights which are already available to men but in their existing form and without accounting for their gendered realities. Furthermore, although the distribution of sanitary pads and toilets increases girl students' attendance rates and self-confidence in class, these initiatives (which I clearly support and promote) risk reducing educational solutions for girls to tangible items.[19] What good are sanitary pads and toilets if the educational institution itself is a site of trauma and institutionalized sexism? This focus on tangible items can overshadow the need for larger structural changes in gender relations. Structural changes are an important prerequisite for improving the net achievement of all students, but especially girls.

Even if girls attain high academic marks and greatly increased access to educational institutions, this does not mean that equity has been achieved.[20] It does not mean that schools, and for that matter society, have eliminated sexism. In fact, it does not mean much at all if girls and women are subsequently prevented from controlling their life trajectory.

Schools, therefore, must be guided by a shared mission or value system around the education of girls. This mission cannot be one of assumed understanding, based on blanket references to equality between men and women. It must be a mission that specifies the role of power in defining gender relations and then works toward its destruction through changes in institutional policies, practices, and general culture. Gender-sensitive schools, in their traditional conception, do not do this.

Defining Gender Equity as Liberation

In her book *Teaching to Transgress*, bell hooks emphasizes the importance of teaching critical thinking as a mechanism to enable students to transgress gender confines, thereby enabling equity and ultimately liberation: "Education as the practice of freedom is not just about liberatory knowledge, it's about a liberatory practice in the classroom."[21] Her work focuses on liberation as a pedagogy that can incite the interests of students and transform them into active learners who believe that the content of the knowledge they consume is socially meaningful.

For a school to consciously engage in practices enabling liberation, it must embody "an idea of change that dismantles unequal power relations."[22] It requires an explicit and intentional acknowledgment of gender and the ways in which it shapes socioeconomic inequity.[23] It requires schools to teach girls not only how to deal with challenges but also how to reshape them, subvert them, destroy them, and reconstruct them. In sum, for schools to take on the work of equity and thus liberation, they must disrupt inequitable power relations and redistribute them. Institutions that do this work are not simply friendly to girls or sensitive to gender. They are feminist schools.

Becoming a Feminist School

In short, feminism refers to equality of both sexes. Given the various connotations—both negative and positive—associated with the term *feminism*, it may be valuable to clarify what I mean by using the term *feminist schools*. Broadly, when I reference feminism, I am incorporating elements from all the various existing forms of feminism—classic feminism, Black feminism, Third World feminism, womanism, Africana womanism—because, as it has been pointed out, "it is necessary to think of a plurality of feminisms and emphasize the diversity of women's experiences."[24] The feminism that I refer to in this book embodies the need to enact anti-racist, anti-sexist, and thus liberatory practices and ideologies.[25]

In thinking about what feminist schools look like, my central premise is that schools should act not as microcosms of society, but as models of equity. Schools can act as models of equity by engaging in practices that ensure all burdens are shared fairly and that innate biological differences in sex—to a first approximation—are accounted for.

Feminist schools protect children from threats that impose a differential cost on their ability to secure equivalent net achievement. These threats can be related to infrastructure, or they can be social, physical, sexual, or economic elements. For example, feminist schools know it is unfair for a girl to work two years and save while her parents fund her brother's schooling, or for a girl to monitor how she dresses to avoid harassment and assault by male teachers because of a characteristic she cannot control (that of being a girl).

Feminist schools assess and evaluate the gender equity of institutional practices, from hiring to instruction, and then develop targeted interventions based on the results. They design curricula that strip restrictive gender roles from homework questions or sample word problems and instead implement those that emulate the overlapping identities of gender, race, and class by which those most marginalized identify. They educate girls on their rights related to issues such as sexual abuse, empower girls to report when their rights are violated, and institute measures to ensure they are not rebuked for it.

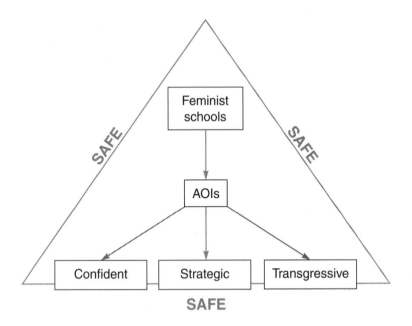

FIGURE I.I. How feminist schools shape achievement-oriented identities

Most important, feminist schools are attentive to the power dynamics that shape students in the classroom. In doing so, they disrupt power relations and provide girls with the tools to do the same in the many contexts they will traverse thereafter. They encourage the use of democratic educational practices by ensuring members of the school community are responsive, respectful, and representative. They act as safe spaces, thereby creating a climate of tolerance and full acceptance of gender fluidity. Finally, they enable students to transgress traditional gender practices, thereby encouraging young people to transition from passive learners to active agents of social change. Students can then emerge from school with the skills needed to respond to hostile environments and defend themselves through the construction of what I call *achievement-oriented identities* (AOIs).

Constructing Achievement-Oriented Identities

In the following chapters I will explain how feminist schools construct achievement-oriented identities, defined as positive beliefs in individual abilities and the facility to translate those beliefs into realizable actions.[26] Achievement-oriented identities, or AOIs, are not reflective of any single trait, such as grit or self-control, but rather encompass a set of traits, primarily those of self-confidence, strategy, and transgression. Feminist schools provide students with practical and emotional tools useful for developing AOIs. Such schools help students construct them through their practices, policies, and general culture. Evidence of these identities can be seen in students' positive attitudes toward learning and strategic behavior toward challenges they confront.

The concept of achievement-oriented identities must account for the gendered nature of the challenges faced by girls. Undoubtedly, schools play a significant role in the process of upholding and upending norms and thus act as key engines of gender socialization. Most commonly, schools' various practices send cues to students about gender based on traditional conceptions of masculinity and femininity. For example, when students are separated by gender in class, sports, and other recreational activities, they are often being trained to act in ways that align with gender stereotypes found in society rather than making room for diverse gender expression.[27]

In response, the school that produces achievement-oriented identities among its girl students builds their self-confidence, shows them how to behave strategically, and encourages them to transgress societal norms. The development of these skills is facilitated by feminist schools that intentionally dismantle the intersecting race and gender barriers constraining girls, thus protecting them from harm. In doing so, feminist schools provide students with the proper social conditions to experience net achievement and build achievement-oriented identities. Girls can then use their newly formed skills to move toward power (or rather disrupt power) globally.

Maximizing the Potential of Every Student

I have written this book to recenter gender equity in debates on global education reform as a mechanism to maximize human potential, now and in the future. It is more than an empowerment narrative about girls.

However, in focusing on girls, I have two primary objectives. One objective is to emphasize how the educational experiences of girls have been undermined by limited measures of assessing achievement, measures that reify gender inequity. In making this point, I also offer the idea of net achievement as an inclusive concept that accounts for institutional sexism and the direct and immediate ways in which it continues to constrain students' life chances.

Another objective of the book is to put forth a theory of feminist schools and the construction of achievement-oriented identities. In proposing feminist schools, my goal is to promote institutions that ensure girls have positive and equitable experiences, regardless of their academic ranking. I make the case that a feminist school's ability to produce positive and equitable experiences for its students creates the conditions necessary for students to construct achievement-oriented identities. These AOIs teach girls how to successfully engage with a world that is inequitable and thus hostile. In short, feminist schools protect girls now, and then provide girls with the tools—AOIs—to protect themselves and others in the future.

With that said, the notion of achievement-oriented identities is *not* meant to be a trickle-down strategy. Instead, it is what I view as the ultimate product required in any remediation:

acknowledgment. The construction of AOIs requires schools to acknowledge the inevitable barriers along the lines of gender that students will face and to provide proactive redress. But such measures are necessarily short term. They will not eliminate sexism in society; they only respond to it. The long-term solution is for society to become a more equitable place. Still, feminist schools that help students develop achievement-oriented identities contribute to this effort in important ways.

Schools must answer difficult questions in order to transform themselves into feminist institutions that promote achievement-oriented identities:

- How does our refusal to address gendered barriers in our educational practices constrain our ability to serve all students equitably?
- How can we expand what we mean by *achievement* to include not only equitable academic outcomes but also equitable educational experiences for all genders?[28]
- How can we expand discussions around "quality schools" to include gender and make gender central to the education reform process?

How Girls Achieve answers these questions through an academic investigation of the experiences of girls who attend schools in South Africa, Ghana, and the United States—all countries that have an explicit commitment to achieving gender equality. As shown in the analysis, South Africa is a middle-income country where boys and girls attend most levels of school at equivalent rates but where issues at the intersections of race, poverty, and violence exacerbate negative educational experiences. The United States is a high-income country where the overall rate of girls accessing education surpasses that of boys, and yet the country also contends with serious and persistent racial and socioeconomic inequities. Ghana is a low-income country where poor girls attend higher levels, or grades, of school at lower rates than boys. Across these case studies, achievement-oriented identities are discussed as a mechanism for developing policy solutions that circumvent barriers for girls in both the developed and developing world. From my analysis, the importance of developing feminist schools that produce achievement-oriented identities is revealed.

Chapter 1 expands the theory through an analysis of how schools facilitate the learning of young girls from poor households in the middle-income country of South Africa, where girls attend school at similar rates to boys but where both race and economic disadvantage intersect with gender. Despite South Africa's economic prowess on the continent, its educational system is known as one of the worst in the world.[29] As the country's most vulnerable population, poor Black girls are especially at a disadvantage. Utilizing qualitative data on Cape Town, South Africa, I profile one of the most successful schools serving the poorest communities. This school facilitates the successful learning of populations facing high levels of violence. In centering the stories of girls who perform at high levels academically, I highlight the danger of focusing on grades as an indicator of achievement. How do schools ensure girls' net achievement when educational spaces may be unsafe? This chapter examines what it takes to create safe spaces for girls, and how these spaces encourage the formation of AOIs and feminist schools.

Chapter 2 brings these conversations to the United States, with a focus on the achievement of Black girls at a single-sex school in a large, urban school district. Disadvantaged Black girls in the United States have access to education but suffer from negative educational experiences that intersect with race, gender, and poverty. By focusing on a context where girls perform at higher levels relative to others, I explore the power of feminist practices for propelling students toward not only net achievement but also social change. How do schools promote net achievement, achievement-oriented identities, and social change while serving a population with intersecting disadvantages? Chapter 2 explores how feminist schools may address these concerns.

Chapter 3 returns to Africa, to a typical urban school in Ghana, where we see the theory of achievement-oriented identities in practice. In the developing country of Ghana, poor girls attend school at lower rates than boys. The girls we meet in this chapter are striving to be the first in their families to go to college.[30] These identities promote not only self-efficacy and confidence but also strategy and transgression, thus acting as protective factors against the specific gender-related challenges impeding the girls' ability to succeed in the future. How can a feminist school affect the achievement-oriented identities of girls even after they leave the schoolhouse? In Chapter 3, I explore factors that can protect students not only at school but when they leave school.

The findings in these three chapters have practical implications for reducing educational inequities across class, gender, and school quality, in both developing and developed countries. Nonetheless, these findings largely overlook established research on noncognitive skills and traditional measures of academic achievement. How should we weigh noncognitive skills? How do these skills relate to academic performance in the context of feminist schools and achievement-oriented identities?

Chapter 4 examines the limits of confidence and other noncognitive skills. I work with data on standardized scores and attitudes toward math and science in South Africa, the United States, and Ghana. The data examine how confidence—a key aspect of achievement-oriented identities—and socioeconomic background work together to shape the academic performance of girls across these various contexts. These data show why confidence and other noncognitive skills, which AOIs emphasize, are by themselves insufficient measures of achievement, academic or net. Rather, girls need feminist institutions that eliminate the gendered barriers they face and teach them the strategies they need to respond to barriers thereafter. Noncognitive skills have their limits when they are used to address structural poverty across diverse countries. Feminist schools are essential to securing equitable net achievement.

In the Conclusion I summarize the empirical findings and their contributions to current research on the education of girls globally. I highlight how a focus on educational access and performance ignores negative and inequitable experiences that occur when girls are actually in the classroom. While access to school for girls across the globe is important, as is the need to secure high grades in school, girls must also have positive and equitable educational experiences to ensure that they may thrive beyond the classroom. Feminist schools take actions to mitigate the inequitable costs girls absorb while striving to thrive, and in doing so, define an institutional solution to the problem of gender inequity.

For Girls, and to Those Who Nurture Them

I make it a point to engage primarily in methods that enable a deeper dive into the educational environments in which girls participate routinely. Accordingly, I conducted in-depth qualitative interviews and ethnographic observations, compared and tested against data collected by others. I have emphasized studies that are accessible online, thereby encouraging replication.[31]

I largely avoid discussions on how these findings apply to boys directly. By concentrating on the most marginalized group, low-income girls, we can develop solutions that will help all students achieve. Although I devote my attention to marginalized girls, if boys are safe from the confines of toxic masculinity in a feminist school, they should be more liberated to act feminine of center as well. I discuss class, disability, sexuality, and mental health, but these are by necessity not the focus of this book. Future research is needed in this regard. I hope this book will spur others to think about gender broadly in the very practice of education equity, and that those who live and do this work might take up where I leave off—and be kind about it.

As a Black woman studying mostly Black environments, I found that it was relatively easy to eliminate research subjects' fear around the intent of the research. Nonetheless, I also had to be intentional about my own preconceptions to ensure the systematic nature of the data collection and analysis. These data are in no way perfect, but they are an accurate portrayal of what I observed about the educational experiences of girls over the years and the commonality of those experiences across different countries. Thus, the solutions proposed should be those most necessary to enable students to have equitable access to net achievement.

Throughout the book, my focus on the experiences of poor Black girls is intended to broaden, not limit, the scope of my work. Much of the literature on the relationship between gender and educational achievement addresses the experiences of White women and girls, and thus completely fails to address the experiences of everyone else. Because poor Black women and girls often occupy the most marginalized positions across global contexts, focusing on their narratives allows us to think about feminism as inclusive of dismantling multiple systems of oppression—racism, classism, and sexism—thus creating a more equitable society for all people.

At this point, it is important that I clarify what I mean by the term *girl*. The term is often fraught. While there are biological elements to one's sex, gender is constructed based on societal context. This book is very clearly about those who possess a uterus. But it is also about those who are perceived to be "girls" based on traditional notions of gender. This distinction is an important one, as the book is premised on the assumption that society is hostile toward those who, biologically speaking, are not or are not perceived to be boys or men. I am concerned specifically with the social impact of being a "girl," based on these preconceived ideas. By using the term *girl,* I refer first to children with "female-gendered bodies" because there are baseline commonalities in the challenges they face irrespective of their sexuality or gender identification. But I am also addressing children who express so-called feminine traits irrespective of their physical body-gender.[32]

Nonetheless, I am fully aware that heteronormativity and cis-male privilege continue to constrain our actions every day, even as we seek to build more equitable institutions. I have no doubt that even as I have tried to write my way out of these constraints, at various times in this book I have slipped right back in.[33] Still, my aim for the reader is the same: to understand the challenges that traditional conceptions of gender pose for girls; to conceive how schools can and should respond to them to create a feminist environment in which all students can thrive; to imagine how schools can be and should be models for democratic institutions generally; and to comprehend how the status of girls, not only in terms of educational access and performance but also in terms of general well-being, is a measure of society's ability to live up to its promise.

Finally, I must remark on who this book is for: I write *for* girls and *to* parents, policy makers, educators, organizers, academics, and administrators. I hope the conception of school as a shelter for the minds and bodies of girls exposed to a world that would consume them incites them to build. I write to offer a seed for those on the ground, that they may alter it to fit their needs and give it life. I write this as a scholar because my colleagues have done their utmost to catalog inequity, and I believe now is the time to offer a vision of how to proceed. If this is not the path forward, I hope it is the first step.

One

Becoming Safe

Please teach your daughters not to measure their
strength by how much pain they can endure.

—SANUSI

ZENEBA IS A South African success story.[1] The twelfth grader is
ranked among the top ten of her graduating class at the Wellsboro School, one of the best government schools in South Africa.
When she graduates, her plan is to study medicine at one of the
country's most highly ranked institutions, the University of Cape
Town.

Zeneba is Black and Muslim. Born in 2001, she was raised in
a poor neighborhood right outside of Cape Town by a single
mother. Her achievements would have been impossible barely
twenty years ago under an apartheid system that explicitly limited the opportunities of Black South Africans. For many poor
Black Muslim girls from her hometown, Zeneba's success still is.

So, how did Zeneba beat the odds? How did she, unlike most
of her peers, overcome the barriers stacked against her to achieve
academic success? But to ask—and answer—that question would
be to undermine Zeneba's telling of her own story: "I don't have
the best home life. I don't get tutored like half the students on
the top ten list. They don't have all these extra chores . . . The

other Black student . . . Her home life is also harder . . . We have to work twice as hard."

Being poor and being Black are not the only obstacles to education Zeneba faces. She goes on to discuss her concern with gender. "Although women are on par in terms of academics [in South Africa], there is still stigma because ultimately the social and power dynamics haven't changed . . . No matter how successful I will be as a doctor, they are still going to be an incessant voice that this is the time I need to be married." Indeed, Zeneba knows she is an excellent student, and is confident in her ability to become a medical doctor. Still, she chose to spend most of our time together in 2017 talking about her challenges at school. In particular, she talked about the barriers faced by people of her race, income, and gender, emphasizing her need to "work twice as hard" as her White and Coloured peers, and explaining the stigma of not being married like her Muslim classmates.

Zeneba is not alone in her concerns.

Her classmate Kai, "the other Black student," is also one of the top ten students in the class. "My grades are really good. They are excellent," Kai told me in our interview in 2017. Yet, Kai's description of their work life echoes Zeneba's.[2] "I have to study way before most people. I work after school, so I don't have time to really do [home]work. I do my studying on the train, in class. I don't get much sleep at home because while other people are sleeping I have to do work. I go to sleep at 10 or 11 P.M. and then wake up at 3 A.M." Like Zeneba, Kai is also concerned about gender: "I find it difficult to identify with one of these genders. My gender is not represented at a coed school. I want my gender and my sexuality as queer and nonbinary to be represented at the school, but it's not . . . I wouldn't say school is a really safe space."

Zeneba and Kai come from similarly poor backgrounds and are academically successful. Yet they feel a lack of safety at their school. These feelings, explained in more detail later, are strongly linked to their experiences with race, class, and gender disadvantage. Taken as a whole, their feelings and experiences make clear that academic success does not guarantee safety. Zeneba and Kai, like all students, need and deserve more than just academic success. They need and deserve safe schools.

To let girls learn, schools must first protect them.

Developing a Safe School

Prior work has defined a safe school as "one that is free of danger and . . . absen[t] of possible harm; a place in which all learners may learn without fear of ridicule, intimidation, harassment, humiliation or violence."[3] Unfortunately, most existing schools do not operate as safe spaces. Instead, schools typically host and sponsor dedicated safe-space programs within and around them.

Safe-space programs in school communities are typically only for girls and meet several times a week in public places like community halls and youth centers. They are run by girls or women who are slightly older and from the same community as the girls themselves. These mentors develop a loose curriculum, including topics such as sexual and reproductive health and gender-based violence. They teach "safety plans" or other life skills, such as financial literacy and civic engagement.

In addition to the knowledge gained from participating in one of these programs, girls also gain role models and a social network of peers they can trust. Trust is especially important for girls as they are typically less likely to have mutually reciprocal peer relationships compared with boys. In fact, studies conducted on South Africa reveal that 33 percent of girls do not belong to a community group, and that 43 percent of girls but only 19 percent of boys describe themselves as not having friends.[4] Research on select safe-space programs finds that girls who have participated in them are not only more likely to report feeling more socially included but also more likely to save money and report an increased understanding of sexual violence.[5]

Still, safe-space programs are insufficient in many ways. The stigma of being a victim of sexual assault has been shown to prevent girls from reporting these crimes, despite increased understanding.[6] Furthermore, while girls want safe-space programs, home obligations often constrain their ability to attend them, especially at locations outside of school.[7] In summary, even though safe-space programming can potentially empower girl students to speak up and out, their community accessibility and impact on sexual violence are limited by design. Girls need safe spaces that extend beyond a temporary offsite meeting. Put another way, to encourage reporting and attendance, schools must not only support occasional safe-space programs, they must ensure that every area of the school is a safe space.

A school that is entirely safe is a school that values net achievement. I focus here on South Africa, where many students sit at the intersection of race, gender, and poverty. These students voice a need to attend institutions that protect them from the everyday violence associated with those identities. But first, to properly understand the educational experiences of Black South African girls, it is necessary to understand the history of structural disadvantage directed toward them.

Education in South Africa

That South African schools can potentially become safe spaces reflects major progress for a nation that, just twenty years ago, explicitly practiced racial and gender inequality across the education system. It was only in 1996 that the South African government extended equal education to Black Africans, and thus Black African girls, under the South African Schools Act. Before then, during apartheid, the country engaged in a bifurcated education system in which Whites benefited from the highest quality education and resources, while Black Africans were subjected to lower-quality education, detailed in the Bantu Education Act.

The Bantu Education Act was instituted in South Africa in 1953, immediately following *Brown v. Board of Education* in the United States in 1952, which led to desegregation in schools. The Bantu Education Act—later that year renamed the Black Education Act and then finally the Education and Training Act in 1979—was developed to effectively legalize segregation through the development of separate educational facilities for Blacks and Whites in the country. As with schools in the United States before *Brown v. Board,* these facilities were separate and unequal. In fact, it was reported that in 1967 under Bantu Education the ratio of teacher to student in Black schools was as high as 58 to 1 and that spending on Black education was less than 10 percent of what was spent on White education.[8] In 1990, for every $150 spent on a White primary school child, $10 was provided by the state to a Black child.[9]

Segregation in education extended beyond secondary school. In 1959, the Extension of University Education Act was passed, which disallowed Black students from attending White universities, instead setting up "tribal universities" for Black students. As a result, White students were trained for managerial positions, but Black Africans were trained to take on inferior roles in the country.[10] In short, the education system—from early education through university—served the state's racist mission.

Single-sex schools were largely inaccessible to African students and instead reserved for Whites.[11] Once the South African Schools Act was passed in 1996 to reduce racial inequality, single-sex schools for girls were established as a mechanism for protecting them from sexual violence and harassment in addition to improving their knowledge of women's rights. Still, these schools were not created for working-class girls of color. Instead, many Black girls attend formerly all-White girls' schools.[12]

Girls were not legally denied access to education under the apartheid regime. In fact, during apartheid the number of girls enrolled in primary and secondary school was nearly equal to boys. Additionally, girls on average outperformed their male counterparts in the early years of apartheid.[13] Yet, girls faced many gender-based barriers, including sexual harassment and tracking into subject areas based on gender stereotypes. These barriers ultimately inhibited their performance at higher levels of education.[14] Female teachers also earned lower pay and worked only in nonsenior management roles.[15] Altogether, while women had access to education, they struggled to advance academically and continued to occupy inferior positions compared with men in a highly patriarchal public and private economy.

Since 1996, or post-apartheid, South Africa has not only increased its educational investment in African students but has also increased its commitment to gender equality through its constitution (Section 9, specifically). Public spending on education is 6.4 percent of the gross domestic product—more than any other African country and the United Kingdom. Girls continue to attend schools at similar rates to their male counterparts at both the primary and secondary level, and they perform on par with boys in most subjects, except math. Furthermore, more girls than boys take the college matriculation exam.[16]

Despite South Africa's significant investment in education and the development of liberal educational policies, however, its educational system remains one of the worst in the world. In the World Economic Forum's Global Competitiveness Report for 2016–2017, South Africa ranked 138th out of 140 countries in the quality of education.[17] In another study conducted in 2015 by the Organisation for Economic Co-operation and Development, South Africa ranked 75th out of 76.[18] Although these reports applaud South African primary and secondary enroll-ments, they note that only 4 percent of its students earn a college degree. For women and girls, in particular, their academic achieve-ment outcomes have been lukewarm at best. Younger girls en-roll in schools at higher levels than boys on average, but they are less likely to be academically successful while enrolled. At college, women represent less than one-third of those who graduate with degrees in engineering, physics, and computer science.[19] Race, gender, and poverty play an important role in explaining the low levels of academic and net achievement in South Africa.[20]

Barriers Girls Face: The Intersection of Race, Gender, and Poverty

In the early 1990s, Kimberlé Crenshaw, a legal scholar, described the need to understand how marginal identities of race and gender overlap and in turn constrain women and girls. She named this concept *intersectionality.* "My objective there was to illustrate that many of the experiences Black women face are not subsumed within traditional boundaries of race or gender discrimination as these boundaries are currently understood, and that the intersec-tion of racism and sexism factors into Black women's lives in ways that cannot be captured wholly by looking at the race or gender dimensions of those experiences separately."[21]

By examining the compounded effects of race and gender dis-crimination, intersectionality provides a more comprehensive and accurate view of the experiences in which Black women and girls find themselves in the world and, specifically, in school. Elaine Unterhalter, an academic who specializes in the inequalities of race, gender, and class, provides a useful way to discuss poverty as part of race and gender marginality through three metaphors: as a line, a net, and fuel. The *line* refers to efforts to measure equality by counting the number of women and men above a certain threshold (for example, the number of girls in poverty at school compared with boys). This method of measuring poverty and equality, although important for accountability, acts as a crude measure of substance. The *net* refers to the ways in which race, gender, and poverty are meshed into hierarchies of unequal power relations that schools often reproduce and girls internalize. Schools' reproduction of unequal power relations, and girls' internalization of them, are then replicated through a continued sexual division of labor in the household and at work. Unterhalter concludes that instead of seeing gender as a line, one must see it as part of a network of relationships in which race, gender, and poverty interact and intersect. It is only in this way that schools can provide the *fuel* necessary to transform gender relationships. Doing so requires schools to be positioned to reduce inequities—not to reproduce them.[22]

GENDER-BASED VIOLENCE

Understanding how schools can reduce racial, gender, and economic inequities begins with understanding the challenges girls face once enrolled. In South Africa, for example, girls experience high levels of gender-based violence in the classroom. These range from implicit violence, such as corporal punishment and bullying, to explicit sexual violence, such as sexual harassment, rape, and abuse.[23] For example, one study revealed that nearly one in three girls reported being raped in or around their school in South Africa. Of those who reported being raped, 33 percent reported being raped by their educators.[24] A survey of 1,500 youth conducted in 1998, only a few years after apartheid ended, found that 43 percent of girls indicated sexual violence was "very common," and 33 percent of those surveyed said they had personally experienced it at school.[25]

Indeed, significant education policies have been passed to reverse these trends. In 2003, the Ministry of Education in South

Africa formed the Girls Education Movement (GEM) to build knowledge and self-esteem of girls through student-led organizations, ranging from drama clubs to HIV prevention workshops. In 2007, a life orientation and skills curriculum was established in primary schools across South Africa to further instill confidence in girls within the classroom. That same year, Prevention and Management of Learner Pregnancy guidelines were established for girls who wished to return to school if they had left or had been kicked out of school for being pregnant. This policy was followed by additional guidelines, Prevention and Management of Sexual Violence and Harassment in Public Schools, in 2008. Nonetheless, recent research and reports suggest that rape and sexual abuse remain a relatively pressing concern for South African schoolgirls.[26]

MENSTRUAL MANAGEMENT AND SANITATION

Adolescence is a particularly vulnerable time for girls. As they transition through puberty and begin their menstrual cycle, they may find access to sanitary pads and hygienic products challenging. Education about changes they are experiencing may not be readily available. In many environments where access is more difficult, menstruation is viewed as taboo or as a reason to exclude girls from activities. Being able to deal with menstruation effectively directly affects girls' ability to achieve in educational settings. An inability to manage menstruation or talk about it with adult women may lower schoolgirls' self-esteem and self-confidence, discouraging them from attending school altogether.[27]

Beyond a lack of female mentors and girls' health education, many schools simply lack basic facilities. For example, in South Africa's public, non-fee, and paying schools, only 41 percent of students have access to flush toilets.[28] Accordingly, girls may feel both unsafe and uncomfortable attending school for the five or six days out of the month when they have their period. Lack of flush toilets particularly discourages disabled girls who are menstruating from attending school or simply participating in school activities.[29] Yet, girls who miss school are more likely to fall behind and eventually drop out. Thus, simple aspects of school infrastructure, such as access to toilets, can play an important role in helping girls succeed.

HIV / AIDS

In South Africa, 56 percent of the 6 million people living with HIV/AIDS are women and girls.[30] New incidences are most prominent among young women between the ages of fifteen and twenty-five, and the HIV/AIDS incidence rates for girls are higher than for boys overall. As recent as 2013, it was estimated that more than 25 percent of South African schoolgirls were infected, compared with just 4 percent of schoolboys.[31]

Dealing with HIV/AIDS affects the educational experiences of girls specifically. For example, one study found that schools in South Africa with high prevalence rates of HIV/AIDS experienced slightly decreased enrollments of female students due to a loss of support from the death of parents affected by the disease.[32] If families dealing with HIV/AIDS must choose who to send to school among their children, girls are typically excluded because of their traditional roles as caretakers. For girls who have HIV/AIDS, they may miss school if their parents feel that having HIV/AIDS is stigmatizing and want their children to avoid discrimination. Instead of sharing or reporting their experiences, girls dealing with HIV/AIDS, either themselves or through their families, often drop out or suffer in silence for fear that reporting what they experience will result in rebuke from their families and surrounding communities.[33]

Ironically, several studies document the power of education to reduce the probability of a girl being infected by HIV/AIDS.[34] A study conducted in Botswana found that participants were

7 percent less likely to contract HIV/AIDS for each additional year of school they completed.[35] Furthermore, the completion of primary education has been found to translate to a lower probability of engaging in unprotected sex in general.[36]

Nonetheless, many schools in South Africa do not incorporate curriculums that teach about sexual and reproductive health. While life orientation classes are meant to discuss these issues, and do, schools report that teachers are not trained on the particular subject, so the course ends up being randomly assigned to anyone who needs an extra class to teach. This random approach to assigning a teacher to a course likely affects the way the course is perceived among teachers and students, and negatively impacts the consistency with which the course is taught. In addition, improperly framed health education can serve to further silence students if restrictive constructions of gender are reproduced and perpetuated. Certain ideas about gender—for example, that men should keep their problems to themselves and, thus, exhibit self-control, or that women's emotions should be policed and, thus, aligned with what men have deemed acceptable—affect the success of interventions that seek to encourage young girls to speak out. Thus, even as education acts as a social vaccine for helping to reduce HIV/AIDS among girls, schoolgirls who are infected or affected need an environment in which girls do not feel ashamed to share what they are experiencing. Policies and programs such as the Girls Education Movement represent an important contribution to solving this issue, as they facilitate an environment in which achievement-oriented identities can be instilled. Yet, it remains critical for schools to act as the central space in which strategies may be developed to help girls deal with and respond to their challenges.

At the very least, schools can impart lessons on how to navigate difficult educational experiences while working to improve them. At best, schools can begin as safe spaces that provide students with opportunities to learn skills they can use to transgress in an unsafe world. In other words, safe schools can provide the conditions necessary for teaching students to navigate educational barriers. Kai and Zeneba at the Wellsboro school in Cape Town, South Africa, had much to tell me about their own achievements and the pitfalls they encountered on the way.

Wellsboro: Striving to Create a Safe School in the Western Cape

In 2014, in collaboration with members of the Human Sciences Research Council, I investigated schools in South Africa that serve mostly disadvantaged students and yet are successful in transforming them into academically successful learners.[37] In 2017, I returned to South Africa, specifically the Western Cape province. Known for being a relatively wealthier area in South Africa, the province boasts the second highest median household income in the country. It is also one of the most educated regions in the country, with a high school graduation rate of 80 percent. In terms of academic performance, students in the Western Cape consistently score among the highest in the country relative to students in other provinces. It is also home to one of Africa's best universities, the University of Cape Town. Nearly 50 percent of learners from the Western Cape scored at or above the average for science (400) in data collected by the Trends in International Mathematics and Science Study (TIMSS) in 2015. Western Cape students are also more likely to report having books at home and their own math and science textbooks at school, and least likely to report bullying compared to any other province. While the educational level of households actually decreased by 8 percentage points between 2003 and 2015, the Western Cape still represents one of the relatively wealthier and more educated provinces in South Africa.[38] My investigation focuses on how a government fee–paying school in Cape Town—still a relatively privileged school—struggles to create safe spaces for girls in a changing and challenging environment.

The Wellsboro School was constructed in 2012 in response to a mandate by the government to develop an institution that would serve low-income students from across the province. The goal was to provide them with the highest level of education possible at a fee more than ten times lower than a typical private institution. In 2017, the school boasted gender parity across grade levels and even within the senior administration; it had a matriculation passage rate above 90 percent and a college attendance rate above 75 percent, with girls slightly outperforming all other genders. The school provides many resources, including smart boards in each classroom and access to computers and projectors. It is also located in one of the province's wealthiest suburbs—a relatively safe community environment. Despite opening only a few years ago, the school is often compared to Model C— elite schools previously reserved exclusively for Whites during apartheid—due to its extensive resources and academic excellence. Accordingly, an opportunity to attend Wellsboro for a poor, Black student in South Africa is an important one.

Still, the costs that Wellsboro students absorb to attend the institution remain high. To start, most Black students come from single-parent or -guardian homes (many are raised by their grandmothers), lack access to food, live in shacks, and hold additional responsibilities outside school, such as chores and babysitting. Brock Lee, Head of Department (HOD) for English at Wellsboro, says, "I've visited a couple of our kids who live literally in corrugated iron space about as big as this office with five or six people, and there's a toilet 5 meters away. Some kids don't have electricity at home . . . So many of our kids are . . . possibly not eating for a day or two at a time."

Unsurprisingly, these added challenges contribute to difficulties for these students in achieving academic success. For example, when Mr. Lee was asked what he believed were the keys to academic success at his institution, he responded, "I think the key to the kids that are successful are that they come from the middle class. If you were to ask every Black kid at our school how long it takes them to get to school and compare it with how long it takes the [other] kids to get to school, probably be about an hour difference."

Mr. Lee acknowledges that the costs associated with coming to school are unequal for Black students compared with others, and yet they are expected to achieve the same academic outcomes. Recognizing this imbalance, Kai, who we met at the beginning of this chapter and who is one of the few academically successful Black students at Wellsboro, developed a petition to remove required extramural activities after school that extend the school day from ending at 3:15 P.M. to 4:30 P.M. For kids who take the train to and from school and who work every day, Kai argued, the later time has a negative impact on their ability to study and, thus, be academically successful. Fortunately, Kai's petition passed, and the additional hour is no longer mandatory at Wellsboro. Kai describes successfully passing the policy as their proudest achievement since enrolling at Wellsboro. The success of Kai's petition in part demonstrates the ways in which the school provides a space for students to engage in actions that ensure they have positive educational experiences.

FINDING STRATEGIES AND STRADDLING IDENTITIES

Undoubtedly, Kai's ability to be a leader and earn excellent grades, despite all the challenges, is where most research on disadvantaged students ends. Kai's successful academic performance would seem to indicate that the school met their needs. Yet Kai is a student balancing multiple identities, many of which are marginalized, that have acted as significant disruptions to their education. In particular, Kai has to navigate an environment that is not accepting of their nonbinary gender identification and queer sexuality. Kai recalls sitting on a committee to enact a gender-neutral policy at the school: "I had to go around to the classes to explain what the policy was about. I said . . . this policy doesn't want to distinguish between genders . . . Like today, I felt like a boy so I wore shorts—they've allowed girls to wear shorts but not boys to wear skirts—and the entire class laughed, and I felt really assaulted and I felt my identity was being questioned."

Kai's self-identification as nonbinary is not taken seriously at the school, which in turn constrains Kai's ability to control their own self-expression and personhood. Negative experiences such as these directly impact students' perception of their education overall, even if they are academically successful. Ultimately, these schools need to educate staff and students to become institutions that are accepting of all genders. It is clear that Kai could benefit from the development of strategies to navigate the inevitable challenges they face in this gender-hostile and, thus, unsafe environment.

The need for specific strategies for navigating the challenges that come with straddling multiple marginal identities applies to the case of Zeneba as well. Her life contains complications outside of her academic success. In particular, she has confronted the tension of adhering to her Muslim faith and taking control of her life trajectory: "My views on certain things and my religion are complicated. If I believe and pray five times a day and do the core things, other things are accessories . . . The hijab is important . . . but it's not the most important. It's [about] what you put first. I put first God, my family, and then myself, and then everything else is secondary."

Zeneba acknowledges that her perspectives on education and gender are not always linked to her religious beliefs and practices. Thus, she looks for ways to balance the two. She faces the pressure of knowing that her academic success may be undermined or challenged by the traditional roles expected of her:

"My mom has seven brothers, and they will make these comments like, 'You still haven't cooked,' and 'How are you going to keep your husband?'" To these statements, Zeneba responds, "I would like to get married, but if that doesn't happen, it's not the first thing on my bucket list."

To an outsider, it may seem as though Zeneba's academic success and confidence allow her to navigate these tensions well. However, religion and family expectations continue to create significant conflicts that affect her educational experience. Teachers at the school are aware their girl students deal with these challenges and seek to help girls navigate them. For example, Blake Rowland, an English teacher, said, "We are teaching this play [called] *Nothing but the Truth*. One of the themes that it's scrapping with is how . . . to grapple with respect for your culture and your tradition as well as stepping into a modern world." He continues, "I had girls in my class being completely honest and saying, 'My culture . . . my family [that] I love and respect is telling me that I have to be this particular way, but I'm being told by the media and by you and by the broader world that I can do this and this and . . . what am I supposed to do?' And I'm like, 'I don't know' because . . . you can't just say, 'Forget it! Be the modern woman and you don't have to do [tradition].' Because that is to disrespect centuries' worth of tradition and often . . . valuable and meaningful stuff, and I can see that internally the cogs are turning and they're realizing that this is ridiculously difficult."

By putting on a play that mirrors the multiple identities and conflicting information his girl students must contend with, Mr. Rowland is providing a space for them to, at the very least, reflect on the apparent contradictions they face daily. In addition to teaching curricula that present situations similar to what the students are going through, Mr. Lee, the HOD of English, explained that the school tries to bring in woman role models who traverse the multiple identities that girls in the school represent. Mr. Lee provided the following example: "I have a friend; her name is [Tara Mills]. She's . . . quite a successful actress . . . in quite a few films in Hollywood and lots of high acclaimed theatre in Cape Town. She came to the school in 2014, and I remember the kids were mad for her. She's a Muslim woman."

By bringing in a Muslim woman who can talk about how she straddles her Islamic faith at home versus in public, Mr. Lee is providing a role model who can be useful to the students and thus engaging in an important tenet of culturally relevant pedagogy—"a willingness to nurture and support cultural competence."[39] The need to bring in outside role models might also demonstrate the necessity of having teachers and administrators that come from backgrounds similar to those of the students who attend the school. Teachers and administrators who share the backgrounds of the students may be better able to share how they themselves negotiate the seemingly conflicting terrains of tradition, modernity, race, gender, and poverty. Mr. Rowland acknowledges this possibility when asked about his biggest teaching challenge: "Being White," he responds. When asked to explain, he acknowledges, "I just don't come from their life experience."

The students appear to find the race of the teachers challenging as well. While the school student population is majority non-White, only three of the twenty-six teachers are Black. Before 2017, only one of the twenty-six teachers was Black. Without prompting, Zeneba spoke of the impact of not having teachers that looked like her: "A lot of teachers are White. There are like three Black teachers out of twenty-six, and two came this year, and I feel very intimidated. I change how I talk . . . I feel like they wouldn't be able to understand how I talk . . . The way they teach as well, especially the White teachers, is an advantage to non-Black students, especially in English where it's discussion-based. Like when a Black person raises a concern, it's like we shouldn't get that deep into it. They dampen people['s] voices . . . There is really only one teacher I can talk to comfortably." When questioned, Zeneba notes that this teacher is Black.

Fortunately, Mr. Lee acknowledges the challenge of being "the White man telling them how to speak English," and the students interviewed expressed that they have learned to view him, specifically, as an ally. "At the beginning of the year, I struggled talking to him [because] he is male and White," Kai said. "But one day, I didn't know who to talk to, and I went to talk to [Mr. Lee] and he told me I was going to get through . . . and that [I] have to develop a thick [skin]." Still, they largely consider Mr. Lee as an exception. In addition, although Mr. Lee and others acknowledge the difficulty of being a White male who teaches students how to straddle their multiple identities, they also admit they are unsure what to do about it. In the interim, the girl students struggle to see school as a safe space where, in the words of Zeneba, students can express themselves "openly, without fear of judgment."

EXPERIENCING SEXUAL ABUSE, TRAUMA, AND HARM TO SELF-ESTEEM

Wellsboro students have significant encounters with everyday violence, often in and on their way to school. For example, multiple students shared experiences of sexual abuse and harassment at the hands of male peers. Zeneba recalled experiences of being sexually abused by a family friend and then a boyfriend: "I have been sexually assaulted . . . I have been touched by a family friend, and for a long time I didn't know that what he was doing was wrong, and for a while I didn't know it wasn't my fault— from school, religion, from a lot of factors in my life . . . I felt like it was my fault . . . and it happened again later. I had a boyfriend earlier this year, and he wouldn't take a no for an answer, and I was screaming."

Like many girls around the world, Zeneba had not been taught that she did not deserve unwanted sexual advances, and, thus, she found it difficult to see herself as other than blameworthy. She described how school rules to "wear long skirts" to "not invite negative attention" gave her the impression that she should "feel guilty for being a woman." In addition, she described her experiences as contributing to her fear of men: "Now, I don't want people touching me, which is sad because I don't want to be that way."

Similarly, Kai described being sexually abused by two boys at the train stop on their way home from school: "In primary school, I think I was in grade 6 or 5, there were these two boys . . . They bullied me quite a lot. We were at the station, [and] they just felt they were entitled to my body and started to touch me in all the places I did not feel good about. I couldn't really scream anything . . . They told me not to scream."

This was not Kai's only encounter with one of the boys. Kai said, "In grade 8 and grade 9, one of the same boys was asking me out and . . . I said no . . . and he said if he sees me in public he would rape me . . . I had a period where I did not go out my house. It was like a month or so because I was afraid . . . Until this day I still fear for my life . . . It's created a lot of fear in me . . . and it's also scarred me in having relationships with boys."

The effects of these experiences on Zeneba and Kai may not be reflected in their excellent grades, but they are reflected in their lives and, thus, cannot be understated. For both Zeneba and Kai, these experiences negatively affect their perceptions of and relationships with men. They have also led to negative perceptions in regard to their self-esteem and body image. It made them feel guilty for others' actions for which they were not responsible. How can schools work to change this?

Building Achievement-Oriented Identities at Wellsboro

Fortunately, during my research and after there were multiple policies and practices at Wellsboro that sought to improve the educational experiences of students like Kai, thereby contributing to the construction of achievement-oriented identities. These include a greater emphasis on developing a gender-conscious curriculum through Life Orientation and English classes, the establishment of a gender-neutral uniform policy followed by the proposal for a gender-neutral hair policy, and, finally, the promotion of after-school peer networks and trauma-informed counseling services.

SEEKING GENDER-CONSCIOUS CURRICULUMS

In South Africa, all learners are required to take a Life Orientation course in which they learn about important topics, such as sex education. Wellsboro utilized this course to address significant issues related to sexual abuse and rape, which were occurring in and around the school. Mr. Lee described how he set the stage for these conversations by being "open emotionally" and vulnerable. He and other teachers worked to ensure that their education materials do not perpetuate negative gender stereotypes. For example, they discussed an exercise from the required Life Orientation textbook in which students were provided a scenario of a girl student who went to a party and was raped. The exercise then asked students to provide potential reasons for why she was raped. The teachers identified this as an example of victim blaming, so they contacted the administration and publisher and were able to get the exercise removed. Even when the textbook was not explicitly blaming the victim, teachers had to manage how students responded to lessons on rape in co-ed classes, in which students may have "traditional mindsets around what it means to be a man and what it means to be a woman." For example, when learning about rape in Mr. Lee's course, Kai shared the following story: "We had a [Life Orientation] class. We were talking about rape, which was the first time we talked about rape . . . A boy raised his hand and said, 'If a prostitute is raped, is that rape or shoplifting?' and I went up to him after school and I told him, 'You don't understand what females are going through and if your mom got raped, would you like that?' And he said, 'Rape is rape, it just happens.'"

Following the incident, Kai spoke to Mr. Lee, who then assured Kai that their perspective was accurate and to continue "to stand against that." This example demonstrates not only the extent to which unhealthy attitudes about rape take shape but also the clear need for courses in schools that provide a means of talking about topics that may be associated with certain myths, stigmas, or taboos at home.

Furthermore, while these conversations can be, and often are, hurtful at first, they may ultimately lead to a healthy discussion between students on issues such as rape and sexual abuse. Kai said that, after talking to Mr. Lee, they were able to talk to the male student and come to a better understanding on the topic of rape. Kai also mentioned that, thereafter, they were able to more easily engage in healthy discussion on other important issues.

While these conversations may not contribute to increased math scores or traditional forms of academic achievement, Mr. Lee recognizes they are just as important as those measures. In particular, he states: "I'm not doing this to get the marks for achievement. I'm doing it because we live in a culture where . . . a rape happens every five seconds. [There are] horrible statistics of domestic gender violence, and I see it on a daily basis . . . I see patterns of . . . everyday sexism . . . that I find abhorrent. My motivation for doing it is not results driven, it is socially driven."

Students recognize Mr. Lee's efforts to make the school a safe space where they feel protected, which is a critical first step to building achievement-oriented identities. But further work is needed to shape the school as a safe space, in particular the proposal and implementation of gender-neutral policies.

ESTABLISHING GENDER-NEUTRAL POLICIES

When Wellsboro opened, it had specific policies on how boys and girls should dress and wear their hair. Boys wore shorts and girls wore skirts; boys had short haircuts and girls tied up their hair. Before I visited in 2017, these policies were being questioned by the students and administrators alike. For example, Zeneba described how teachers "police" their clothing by "literally measur[ing] how long [their] skirts are" on a routine basis, while Kai discussed their negative experiences with natural hair worn in an afro. As Kai noted, "The teacher told me to tie up my hair because it was untidy. I have an afro . . . my hair is natural. I really like my hair. I didn't tie up my hair . . . It grows outward, it grows up . . . it defies gravity."

Students view school policies related to hair and dress as demeaning. Fortunately, the school worked to implement a gender-neutral uniform policy that was ultimately passed. It then proposed a gender-neutral hair policy that was in the process of being considered at the time of the research. As part of the decision-making process, both students and staff were assigned to a committee on the policy change, and serious discussions were had about what it really meant to ensure that the policy was "neutral." An example of these conversations was reiterated by Mr. Lee: "As it stands now, [the hair policy states that hair] has to be natural color, can't fall down your face, has to be tied up, has to be the same color, and boys have to wear their hair just cut down—neat and presentable . . . And the point was raised by another staff member that hair needs to be considerate of others . . . So if you have afro hair, you are basically [being told] that you can't wear an afro. If the motivation is to let kids be free, should we have a hair policy at all?"

This dialogue highlights how the members of the school struggle to develop a policy that enables students to be free of binaries while still working to be "considerate" of others. Kai, who sits on the committee, holds true to the position that there should not be a hair policy at all by raising the question, "Why would my hair affect my grades?" In the meantime, students essentially hide aspects of themselves while trying to follow the policy in place. For example, Zeneba revealed that she wore her hijab in part to cover the blue dye she put in her hair, while Kai wore bigger glasses to cover a nose ring. Both students were dealing with the constraints of these gender-based policies and working to navigate them and transgress them altogether.

EMPLOYING SCHOOL RESOURCES

When girl students transgress gender-based polices in and outside of the classroom, they still rely heavily on the resources available to them through the school. These resources might seem disparate, from counseling services to sanitary pads. In many cases their most important resource is each other. The availability of counseling services, specifically, is consistent with current efforts to mainstream practices which recognize that kids have serious experiences with trauma, and that this trauma may be exacerbated by punitive school environments.[40] Accordingly, supporters of trauma-informed schools call for an educational structure that is responsive to these traumas at all levels.[41]

At Wellsboro, the availability of a counselor is essential, especially among the many students who describe themselves as coming from backgrounds where they are told to just "deal with it." Kai, for example, had the even greater challenge of balancing achieving academic success and fighting negative educational experiences with battling anxiety and depression. As Kai said, "People are so focused on getting high grades and competition, worried on what is going on on Instagram instead of the world, and it is hard . . . The school does not give me strategies. It's only about working harder and longer, which I do not like . . . I would force myself to study even through my anxiety and depression . . . My emotions fluctuate a lot . . . if I am too happy, then I have a month of going through a lot . . . and I feel numb and empty and I have suicide episodes. I have to stop putting too much pressure on myself so I do not get an episode."

Kai's words make clear the serious challenges of dealing with depression and anxiety in a competitive setting where students are being told that "working harder and longer" is the solution to academic success. Indeed, Kai has confidence, which acts as an important precursor to achievement-oriented identities. However, Kai and other students still need an institutional setting where they can feel safe and have specific strategies to respond to their experiences.

Kai praised the counselor at the school for giving them tools to encourage positive thinking at moments when Kai is considering self-harm. These tools include journaling about happy moments for ten minutes a day to shift their thinking. The counselor's office, thus, is considered a "safe space" where Kai and others can share their challenges and learn how to respond to them.

In addition to counseling, Wellsboro provides another key resource to its girl students: free sanitary pads. The girl students acknowledge that "in most schools, [students] don't have that right." Accordingly, students at the school regularly host drives through the student organization to ensure that those who come from families where they cannot afford pads can have access to them at any time. In addition, they focus on the collection of sanitary pads, as opposed to tampons, after realizing that the use of tampons might exclude their Muslim peers, who may be concerned about "inserting something between their legs." The students' ability to collect resources that consider the financial and cultural cost associated with being a girl on her menstrual cycle is critical for supporting their collective net achievement.

Still, there are perhaps no relationships more important for students than the ones they have with each other. By working with one another, students make clear how their peer-to-peer relationships play a critical role in facilitating their net achievement. For example, during separate interviews, Zeneba and Kai referenced each other multiple times. As stated by Zeneba, "I see a lot of myself in [Kai]. [They] go through a lot of the same things I do . . . [Kai] is cool . . . is very vocal and also does really well in school." Similarly, Kai describes Zeneba as "amazing." She continues, "Some of my motivation is from her . . . I have learned so much from her. She is also one of the reasons I got into journaling." Such positive peer relationships offer one more avenue of support in girl students' educational experiences.

Does Wellsboro Combat Challenges, Protect Girls, and Create Safe Spaces?

The Wellsboro School promotes a clear, gender-conscious curriculum that contends with serious issues such as rape, offers protections such as the promotion and passage of gender-neutral policies, and supplies trauma-informed counseling services and opportunities for peer networking. The school proactively works to provide a safe space where students feel protected. The school's actions also help them develop the strategies they need to confront challenges and transgress norms.

Nonetheless, the school admits that there is much more work to be done. For example, the school has engaged in an increasingly Eurocentric literature curriculum that primarily focuses on

Shakespeare. Additionally, even with the knowledge that kids struggle with food, lights, and transportation, there have been very few specific strategies in place to provide help beyond advice that emphasizes the importance of "working hard." The HOD and other teachers have suggested initiatives such as home visits and department cultural intelligence workshops, but they lacked buy-in because of the general emphasis on math and science at the school.

More broadly, initiatives to fix gender relations as a mechanism for creating safe spaces in all schools across South Africa continue to be stifled by a culture of silence. This culture of silence affects women's and girls' ability to speak about their sexual health, express their vulnerabilities, and make demands for what they need to lead healthy lives. As stated by Robert Morrell, South African scholar and executive director of the Human Sciences Research Council, "Silence is a suppressed discourse. It is thus an effect of power. Dominant discourses permit and [legitimize] certain vocabularies and values while marginalising or silencing others."[42] bell hooks, a leading race and gender scholar in the United States, describes the effect of this silence as "engendered by resignation and acceptance of one's lot."[43] The multiple marginal positions in which girls find themselves often contribute to the perception that they do not have the liberty to share their experiences and be taken seriously. In other words, not all students are as open as Zeneba and Kai about their negative experiences and trauma. In fact, most students aren't open at all.[44] But why should they have to be when they attend schools that fail to provide them with the safety and security to share what they are going through?

As emphasized by advocates of trauma-informed schools, students should be able to have their negative experiences and traumas addressed and accounted for not only at the counseling office, but also in every area of the school. Furthermore, these efforts must take into account the gendered nature of much violence (girls typically experience rape and sexual assault through personal relationships), and that the traumas they produce can have specific, gendered effects (girls are more likely to report anxiety and depression).[45]

Most notably, efforts to transform schools into safe spaces must be developed in concert with revised notions of achievement. In other words, safe schools must contend with the following questions: if Zeneba and Kai earn high grades but experience trauma in the process, have they still achieved? Are they still South African success stories? If not, how can measures of achievement be adjusted to account for a broader awareness of the everyday violence that students face in school?

In the end, academic achievement may be the purpose of a school in an equitable world, but in an inequitable world, a presupposition of a school is that it does not harm its students. Thus, developing a school as a safe space is a critical *first* step to providing all students with the protections they need to secure net achievement. Once schools are safe, they have the foundational components for being gender-equitable—feminist—institutions.

Becoming Feminist

The process begins with the individual woman's acceptance that American women, without exception, are socialized to be racist, classist and sexist, in varying degrees, and that labeling ourselves feminists does not change the fact that we must consciously work to rid ourselves of the legacy of negative socialization.

—bell hooks

As I WALK INTO the cafeteria, the students are quietly eating breakfast.

Once they have finished, the students walk in an orderly, single-file line into the gym. The 200 or so students sit in a circle, each classroom together. Each of the ten classes is named after a university. A student named Bethany runs to the middle and starts to chant:[1]

> We're girls and we matter,
> And we have something to say.
> Are we perfect? No.
> Are we perfect? No.
> We are better today than yesterday.
> Better today than yesterday.

The principal, Donna Knight, takes the lead and yells, "The competition is fierce!" to which the students respond, "The competition is fierce!"

Principal Knight continues: "Who is going to take home Ava [the school's mascot]? Stanford University, we want to hear from you."

A group of about thirty girls sitting in the left corner of the gym begin to chant a song describing their college aspirations: "Reach for the stars . . . I work really hard . . . pocket full of money, on our way to college."

The girls at times hold hands, stomp, clap, and do dance moves, including "dabbing." Some of the harmonies mirror today's newest hits but with the words revised to reflect their personal and professional ambitions.

As the girls chant, their peers and teachers listen, intermittently flashing hands and spirit fingers to indicate comradery. They make no other sound. Principal Knight also provides affirmation as the student's chant.

"Oh, Stanford University had so much [spunk]!" she exclaims.

Each class completes its chant. It takes a total of about thirty minutes. The principal wraps things up by leading the students in the singing of the school song: "We Are the School that Works Hard, and We Will Change the World."

"Who is going [to] take home Ava?" Principal Knight yells again. The students rise and explain why they think they should get to take home the mascot. One group says: "Because we have bright faces and our movements are crisp."

Some even make a case for their friends (or rather, their competition): "Because they have [spunk]!"

The crowd says together: "We like that."

The room is vibrant and spirited but also coordinated and disciplined. No student speaks unless called on. The teachers gather in the circle with the principal, and they discuss the potential winner.

"Brown University," Principal Knight announces. "Now let's get fired up and ready to work."

The students exit the room as quietly and orderly as they entered.

It's time to start the school day.

This is just another ordinary morning at Barbara Teele Elementary, an all-girls K–4 school founded in 2009 by two educators with the lofty goal of increasing the number of women in leadership positions across the United States.[2] Each grade has two classes, and each class has two teachers, allowing a student-teacher ratio of fifteen to one. The school has an extended school day that begins at 7:10 AM and ends at 3:50 PM, Monday through Thursday. On Friday, the day ends at 1:20 P.M. so that teachers can work on professional development. After school and on Saturday, tutoring is also offered.

As of June 2017, the school enrolled 440 students, 90 percent of whom were African American and 73 percent of whom qualified for free or reduced lunch. Of the teaching staff, 60 percent come from historically underrepresented minority backgrounds. Principal Knight is an African American woman who grew up in the same Northeast neighborhood in which the school is located. The area has a population of about 150,000 people, 70 percent of whom are Black and 15 percent Hispanic. The average income is about 37,000 USD per year.

In short, the attendees of Teele Elementary reflect their neighborhood: they are poor students of color—a demographic typically associated with schools that perform the worst academically in the United States. However, despite serving an economically disadvantaged population, Teele Elementary has consistently performed at higher levels than its majority peers at the city and state level. Accordingly, in 2016–17, the school was one out of ten schools in the state to be designated a National Blue Ribbon School—the highest academic distinction for a primary school provided by the US Department of Education.

But does Teele's distinguished academic program alone provide girls with what they need to succeed on their later academic path and, ultimately, in the greater world? I argue that high academic performance is a necessary component, but it is insufficient for the type of schools that girls need. Schools such as Teele Elementary must first engage in practices that keep girls safe. They must then provide girls with tools to develop achievement-oriented identities and, consequently, confidence, strategy making, and the ability to transgress. In doing so, they must serve as models of gender equity. In other words, schools that turn out girls with achievement-oriented identities are, and must be, feminist institutions.

Feminist institutions acknowledge how policies and practices affect boys, girls, and nonbinary identifying students differently, and then proactively respond to those differences. They strive to defy gender norms, as they intersect with race and class, and work to embody equity for all. In their most ideal form, feminist institutions act as sites of social change: they disrupt dominant power structures and redistribute them, thereby ensuring that all students can secure net achievement and contribute to broader societal transformation. In the next section, I provide a brief review of the historical and contemporary state of schoolgirls in the United States before returning to the case of Teele Elementary to illustrate the promise of feminist schools.

The US Educational Landscape

Just over sixty years ago, the US public school system allowed legal segregation of its schools based on race. Although the passage of *Brown v. Board of Education* in 1954 declared segregation unconstitutional, schools in the United States remain highly segregated along the lines of race even today.[3] As the *Brown v. Board* decision became the law of the land, White families fled to the suburbs, thereby effectively resegregating Black families in the city.[4] Consequently, the public-school population shifted from being primarily White to one in which nearly 50 percent of students were of color. Demographic shifts have been associated with major disinvestments in public schools, as they are now filled with students from families with lower levels of resources.[5] For example, one study from the Center for American Progress found that a 10 percent increase in the number of minority students in a school was associated with a $75 reduction in per-pupil spending.[6] This occurs in an environment in which minority students are already half as likely to have a parent who obtained an advanced degree, 23 percent less likely in their childhoods to have a parent who read to them, and three times more likely to be held back a grade when compared with their majority counterparts.[7]

What did the education landscape look like for women and girls just over sixty years ago? Women and girls were underrepresented across every level of education in the United States. If girls did attend school, they frequently went to single-sex schools that emphasized girls' futures as homemakers or at best as secretaries or teachers. When they did attend co-ed schools, they were tracked into fields such as home economics or domestic science. These tracks were especially encouraged for minority girls, even if they had strong academic records.[8]

By 1980, women and men began accessing education at equal levels after the passage of Title IX of the 1972 Education Amendments Act, which bars gender-based discrimination in programs that receive federal funding (20 USC). By 2010, women in the United States represented nearly 50 percent of primary and secondary school enrollment, and 57 percent of college degrees were earned by women (compared to 43 percent by men).[9] That trend has continued at the graduate and doctoral levels.[10]

The Barriers Girls Face in the United States

The relatively high number of girls attending schools in the United States suggests to some that the issue of educational access for girls is no longer relevant and should be deprioritized nationwide. In fact, policies around girls' education passed by US lawmakers are usually intended to assist girl students in developing countries where educational resources are scarcer. The exception is policy regarding recruitment into science, technology, engineering, and math (STEM) education for US girls, such as the 1974 Women's Educational Equity Act. However, even though girls almost universally have access to school in the United States, their educational experiences are often hampered by issues that have gone unaddressed, such as safety and bullying, puberty and pregnancy, mental health and trauma, and school discipline. These barriers, discussed in more detail below, must be addressed for schools to become equitable learning environments.

SAFETY AND BULLYING

In the United States, parents feel relatively secure sending their kids to school every morning, as most assume that their children will be safe while they are there. Indeed, US schools are often touted as "safe havens" and "sanctuaries," even in the most crime-ridden neighborhoods. Given the amount of time young people spend at school each day, one should expect these institutions to be among the safest spaces for children to be.

Yet, youth in America are more likely to be victims of violent crimes than any other age group, and these violent crimes often occur in or around school.[11] In fact, between 2010 and 2013, victimizations at school increased by 100 percent, from twenty

what they think about school, what they think about themselves as scholars, and how they perform as students."[25] For example, a Black girl may begin to believe that she should be able to take on more responsibility than a typical student if she is perceived as mature, and she may be disappointed or ashamed if she is not prepared to do so.[26] This may lead her to ask fewer questions about concepts that are unclear and accept harsher punishments for making mistakes. In addition, research suggests Black girls may act "loud" in order to be seen and heard in spaces where they are typically ignored. The same research notes that girls use this tactic even in African-centered institutions where racial identity is embraced as the norm.[27] Ultimately, it is incumbent on schools to develop constructive experiences and identities for Black girls so that they do not absorb the negative stereotypes typically associated with them.

MENTAL HEALTH AND TRAUMA

Girl students faced with challenges such as abuse, bullying, or negative stereotypes commonly suffer from poor mental health. The Centers for Disease Control and Prevention revealed in 2016 that those who experience sexual abuse and forms of gender-based violence at school have a higher probability of reporting depression, low self-esteem, and suicidal thoughts.[28] In 2009, the National Survey of American Life Adolescent Supplement surveyed more than a thousand African American and Caribbean youths aged thirteen to seventeen years and reported that twice as many Black women (7 percent) attempt suicide before they reach age seventeen compared to their Black male peers. According to the same study, nearly half of those who attempted suicide had not been diagnosed with a mental disorder at the time of the suicide attempt.[29]

In fact, out of the one in five students in the United States who show signs or symptoms of a mental health disorder, only

20 percent receive the mental health resources and services they need.[30] When mental health services are available, the presence of race and gender bias in school shapes how youth learn to manage trauma. Black youth are less likely than their White and Latina peers to receive treatment for mental illness in general, but these numbers are even worse for Black girls because they are perceived as more mature, and thus better able to handle mental health trauma relative to their peers. Accordingly, mental health services, when available, are either offered less frequently to Black girls or Black girls feel less entitled to them (or both).[31]

SCHOOL DISCIPLINE AND PUNISHMENT

School discipline may also act as a mechanism of policing girls' behaviors and bodies to enforce prescribed feminine ways. Although there are higher numbers of incidents of school punishment for boys, research shows that being Black disadvantages girls more.[32] In fact, from between 2002 and 2006, there was a 5.6 percent increase in the number of Black girls being suspended per district, compared with an increase of 1.7 percent for Black boys.[33] Moreover, a 2014 report on school discipline by the US Department of Education's Office for Civil Rights found that Black girls are suspended nationally at higher numbers than all other girls and most boys, even after accounting for the rate of offenses committed.[34]

Regarding how Black girls compare to other girls, research indicates that they typically attend high-poverty institutions where they suffer from disproportionate experiences with school punishment—both in number and severity—compared to their White and Latina peers.[35] A study conducted by the Center for Intersectionality and Social Policy Studies and the African American Policy Forum found that Black girls are ten times more likely to face disciplinary actions such as suspension or expulsion than are White girls, partly due to dominant perceptions of their actions (for example, being too talkative, which is inconsistent with traditional feminine norms).[36] Often, their actions, which may be the same as their peers, are interpreted differently because of preconceived notions steeped in stereotypes of Black girls.

In June 2017, the Georgetown Law Center on Poverty and Inequality released the report "Girlhood Interrupted: The Erasure of Black Girls' Childhood," which was based on a study of 325 adults of different racial and ethnic backgrounds across the United States. Overall, 74 percent of participants were White (and 60 percent of these, or 44 percent of the entire sample, were White women), 11 percent were African American, 7 percent were Hispanic, 4 percent were Asian, and 4 percent were Native American or other. In addition, 39 percent were between the ages of twenty-five and thirty-four, and nearly 70 percent held at least a high school degree. The participants were randomly assigned an equivalent question about a Black girl or a White girl between the ages of zero and nineteen using a five-point scale.[37]

The study revealed that respondents begin to view Black girls as adults when they are as young as five years old, which is five years earlier than for Black boys and significantly earlier than for all other groups. Consistent with previous work, the study titled the phenomenon the "adultification" of Black girls—defined specifically as a process by which Black girls are viewed as more like adults, and thus no longer innocent, relative to White girls of the same age. Because of this phenomenon, the study's authors contend that the public may be less forgiving of mistakes Black girls might make and thus view them as knowingly guilty of their actions. In other words, being viewed as an adult at five years old may deny Black girls the protections—most notably the privilege of innocence—afforded to their majority peers. This perception of Black girls as essentially guilty adults might explain why they are more likely than Whites to be suspended from school and referred to the juvenile justice system.[38]

A Better Educational Experience for Girls

All negative educational experiences—whether related to safety and bullying, puberty and pregnancy, or punishment—faced by Black girl students shed light on the importance of shifting discussions away from an exclusive focus on educational access and performance. Instead, there is a need to prioritize efforts that seek to enable girls to attend feminist schools where they can have positive educational experiences that account for their net achievement.

A school that strives to be feminist must work to first protect its girl students, thereby acting as a safe space that disrupts dominant power relations. Only then can this school impress upon its girl students the achievement-oriented identities that provide them with the power of positive beliefs in their own abilities and the tools to translate those beliefs into realizable actions. Such a school must help girls acknowledge the gender barriers before them and then enable these girls to have confidence in their abilities to respond strategically. Finally, a feminist school must strive to push girls to transgress the traditional norms placed upon them, thereby facilitating their ability to thrive and contribute to societal change.

Toward Feminist Schooling at Teele Elementary

From its leadership to its nonacademic curriculum, Teele Elementary approaches the type of feminist institution necessary for girls to thrive. Teele Elementary benefits from a leadership team that shares both the demographic and household characteristics of its students (60 percent of the faculty are people of color). The students are described by staff as coming from "non-traditional households with two moms or no moms, who face adversities like violence and just being low income." Principal Knight describes herself as growing up in similarly underprivileged circumstances, stating: "I grew up . . . [with] my mom and older sister, and we grew up in a one room house, and my mom's room was in the dining area and we were in the actual [bed]room."

Principal Knight's personal experiences with underserved populations—experiences that are shared by many of her teaching staff—shape her approach to leading the school. When she was in college, she visited a friend who was incarcerated and was struck by how she "went from being on this campus," where she was treated like a deserving student, to this prison, where she was "treated like the scum of the earth." Principal Knight's experience piqued her interest in prison studies, and she soon began a prison tutoring program. Her interactions with one particular inmate played a direct role in developing her interest in teaching: "We were working on simple multiplication facts and he was feeling discouraged . . . and I had to do so much convincing in order to get the buy-in . . . He would be talking about taking care of his kids but he could not do his multiplication, and I am like 'I have to teach' . . . and I have to teach foundational skills and they have to love education, because, as I reflected on my life, it was my educational opportunities that got me here." Similarly, some of her teaching staff were also drawn to the profession because of their direct experiences with underserved populations. One teacher who had been at the school for four years shared the following: "I worked with women on welfare, and a lot of them said that they dropped out of school because they didn't have a person who believed in them. I just thought, 'I wish I got to them earlier,' and that is what brought me to [Teele Elementary]."

The leadership and teaching staff thus came to the school with an interest and genuine passion to work with the type of population Teele Elementary serves. This intentionality has had a positive impact on curating the type of achievement-oriented, feminist institution that Teele Elementary has become.

Instilling Confidence

Perhaps no quality is emphasized more throughout a typical school day at Teele Elementary than confidence. According to Principal Knight, "by teaching our students to persevere, we are building their confidence and assuring them that they can conquer anything they put their minds to." Indeed, she believes confidence is the trait she wants students at Teele Elementary to learn above all others. Many girls arrive at Teele Elementary meek and quiet, she explains, concerned about having perfect handwriting and afraid to disagree. Her goal is to teach students that it is okay *not* to be perfect and that it is okay to have a different opinion. "Part of why you hear them scream their chants [is so they're] not afraid to voice their opinions," Principal Knight explains.

Teachers at Teele Elementary expose students early on to practices that improve their self-confidence. During teacher training, all staff members read "The Confidence Gap," an article published in the *Atlantic* in 2014 that documents how women in the workplace often struggle with notions of perfectionism and thus fail to apply for positions for which they are qualified.[39] By reading articles such as this, teachers begin to understand that nurturing students' confidence will help them meet challenges beyond their school experience. As Principal Knight explains, "When I think about my success, it's not about intellectual ability . . . it's my confidence. We have to make sure every girl here really loves herself, has a strong sense of self-worth, is confident . . . not cocky, knows who they are and can lift others up. We have a unique ability to [do] that in this environment . . . so that is really the goal here, and we see that in their results." Ultimately, Principal Knight acknowledges the specific gender-based concerns affecting the ability of girls to learn, and she works to proactively address them using research as well as her own experience. In doing so, she instills in her teachers a similarly strong belief in the importance of confidence for academic success. As one teacher emphasized, "If these kids have confidence in themselves, they will be able to understand [everything] better . . . that is what will be able to help them to succeed."

I observed teachers integrate these beliefs into their instruction and activities for students. They recognize that students' confidence levels—just like their academic levels—vary, and part of their goal is helping all the students arrive at similar levels. When I asked how they do this, one teacher responded, "It has to do with knowing your kids' strength and highlighting that strength, no matter what that strength is . . . The kid who might be good at math problems, she can build on that . . . I let them show others who they are."

Beyond highlighting the strengths of individual students, teachers assign confidence-building exercises that emphasize persevering through problems and finding "flexible" ways to solve them—a strong element of building achievement-oriented identities. These exercises also emphasize the importance of making mistakes, learning from them, and making a better effort next time. In one assignment I observed, students were asked to reflect on the question, "What makes you confident?" Students' responses reflect an internalization of the lesson being promoted:

> I love my sense of humor and style. I believe in whatever I want to do. I don't care what people think about me. I always try my best.

> I believe in myself all the time even though somebody says I can't do it. I push through. I always say "I can do it" when something is hard.

> I speak loud and proud because my voice matters. I also
> sit up because it shows that I am a strong girl. I raise my
> hand straight to show I am sure of my answer.

This exercise is particularly important for students who experience bullying in school, as one response shows: "I [am] confident in wearing glasses because they make me unique. They help me see. I inspire people with them." Through this activity, the girl is learning how to respond to the challenge of being bullied by reshaping how others view her. Each of the responses is projected on the wall with a picture of the student and her name, thus encouraging girls to embrace what makes them confident in themselves and in each other.

The confidence these girls develop from activities such as this improves their lives inside of school and out. Parents immediately recognize the difference in their children. These parents come to view confidence building as the school's most significant contribution to their daughters' lives. As the mother of a current fifth-grader (and a K–4 graduate) noted, the school gave her daughter "confidence that she wouldn't have otherwise—confidence in just being a girl and knowing that she is fierce and good enough, that she is smart and she got it." She goes on to explain that students at Teele Elementary "think their teachers are everything so they . . . have power and carry a lot of weight [when they tell students] 'you are smart and you can do it, that you are a [womanist woman].'"[40] She continues, "I don't think [my daughter] would have that level of confidence without this school. Thankfully, I don't have to leave that to chance." Clearly, parents recognize that the work of teaching their child extends beyond academics and includes key factors such as confidence. This confidence becomes critical to girls' belief in their ability to persevere when faced with adversity.

AFFIRMATION

Interestingly, I observed that efforts to improve confidence were supplemented by routine affirmation of students. More specifically, Teele Elementary students were provided affirmation for the ways in which they engaged with lessons. I often heard teachers across classrooms say, "Nice straight backs . . . nice going back to the text . . . nice helping hand . . . nice voice." These affirmations were seamlessly woven into class lessons, regardless of the topic, and encouraged students to celebrate not only their intellect but also one another.

In the classroom, for instance, the students "do a lot of self-love building exercises." As one first-grade teacher described, "I found this book about different shades and still being beautiful . . . I have them take out their imaginary mirrors and tell themselves how beautiful they are . . . and highlight in each other the things they think are beautiful."

This affirmation begins as soon as students arrive at school in their morning meeting, as described at the beginning of this chapter, and it continues outside of the classroom as well. For example, students at the school take dance and singing class, which gives them the opportunity to de-stress and learn more about their bodies. They learn and adapt songs that celebrate their belief in their ability to achieve their aspirations, such as the following:[41]

> I'm stepping out, I want the world to know, I got to let
>   it show.
> It's a new me coming out and I am going to live, and
>   I am going to give, I am completely positive.
> I will go to college because I got the knowledge. Oooh
>   I'll pass the test.

Altogether, whether students are told to celebrate their brains, asked to sing about their college aspirations, or given an assignment to reflect on their beauty, their physical and intellectual value are constantly affirmed. This type of affirmation is essential for girls for multiple reasons but especially for building their confidence. One study investigated anxiety among female math teachers, for example. It revealed that girl students enrolled in classes with anxious female teachers were more likely than boys to believe the stereotype that boys were better than girls at math by the end of year. These perceptions also contributed to girls' lower academic achievement.[42] The ability for teachers to provide affirmations for their students, then, may help to explain the high confidence and academic achievement of girls at Teele Elementary.

DISCIPLINE

Another important factor for success that teachers emphasize at Teele Elementary is discipline. As one teacher put it, "The key is confidence and discipline. That is really going to get you to where you want to be, and without that, these [womanist women] have nothing."

The topic of discipline was especially interesting to me because, as explained earlier, Black girls in the United States are often suspended and expelled at high rates compared with all other girls and non-Black boys. Still, discipline is consistently described as a critical factor for enabling girls to achieve academically, not only in the United States but also elsewhere. Thus, I needed to understand how Teele Elementary was using disciplinary practices to achieve positive academic, social, and emotional outcomes.

Teele Elementary has specific rules of conduct that are closely followed by teachers and students alike. There are rules for participation, going to the bathroom, paying attention, reading, raising one's hand, and so on. Principal Knight explained, "We ground our expectations deeply in rationality . . . we don't call out because then we will not be able to hear the things our sister has to say and then we won't be able to build on those ideas."

Indeed, from Day One, students are taught how to behave in a certain way. At times, I was so overwhelmed by the number of rules in place at Teele Elementary that I wondered how many were necessary. Principal Knight noted, "There are many areas throughout the days when misbehavior becomes a teachable moment. Discipline is not the focus of our school. All kids want to do well. All kids want to learn . . . Our teachers work on buy-in from our students."

These statements were echoed by Teele Elementary co-founder Maria Avery, who stated in response to questions about school discipline that "we do everything to keep our kids in schools—we are relentless." She observed that before third grade, girls are relatively kind and well-behaved, but after third grade they begin to bully one another. At Teele Elementary, the staff examines these concerns from the perspectives of social and emotional well-being. "We have had social workers in our school since Year One," Ms. Avery explains. Social workers experienced with aiding students who have been affected by trauma help design responses to misbehavior in class to determine "how students' social and emotional well-being impact[s] their ability to succeed."

When I asked teachers about their strategies for dealing with misbehavior, I heard a variety of long-term as well as short-term solutions. Some of the long-term solutions included changing their approach to the students, changing their tone of voice, considering where and when discipline occurs, and being aware of a student's family background and academic performance. One teacher gave the following example: "I have one student [who] acts out because she is so smart, and she felt like a lot of the work wasn't that challenging, so we thought of additional work we can give her." Long-term discipline involves showing some empathy but also pushing students to be better.

Short-term solutions might include what one teacher calls "the calm down corner." As she explains, "It's not time out. I've told all of [my students] that when you go through something that is hard, you can feel down but you have to come back up . . . and in the calm down corner are a list of calm down strategies . . . you have 5 minutes and if [the anger] has passed and you have calmed down, we welcome you back with open arms."

Strategies to help the student calm down include counting to ten, thinking about their favorite food or color, taking deep breaths, or squeezing a stress ball. If none of these tactics appear to work, the dean of students is called. According to Principal Knight, "we have a culture where [we don't send students out of class] . . . we address the behavior, not the child." The staff seeks to keep the students in school to learn rather than in detention or at home. For example, I observed one incident in which a student was not paying attention, despite the teacher's demands. The teacher, working on guided reading with other students in the class, seemed frustrated. This student appeared to get into trouble often, but she was not kicked out of class. The teacher instead sent the girl's mother a text and showed the student. She then continued the lesson; the student had been disciplined and the learning did not falter. Once the foundational factors of confidence and discipline are in place, Teele Elementary focuses its attention on teaching its students about social justice and how to transgress norms.

Teaching to Transgress: The Development of Womanist Women

Teele Elementary—physically, materially, and socially—reflects the womanist woman curriculum they created to build socially conscious students who transgress norms.[43] In the hallway on the third floor, a poster of Lupita Nyong'o hangs outside a classroom door. It reads: "No matter where you are from, your dreams are valued." Also hanging are images of Toni Morrison and Archbishop Desmond Tutu.

On another wall, there is a long display of *Essence* magazine covers with different images of Black women. Some are actual covers; others were designed by students. Under the display of covers is a description of the magazine's history and the students' reinterpretations of the magazine. There is also a "goals wall" where students state what they want to be: "the first female Mexican president," for example. Outside of the third-grade classroom, a picture of prominent activist Angela Davis appears alongside student letters, one of which reads, "I like how you fought for Black people."

These small details are examples of how the womanist woman curriculum at Teele Elementary works: It connects women role models to specific values, including optimism, respect, honesty, curiosity, justice, love, hope, courage, and sisterhood. Principal Knight explains: "Each month has a . . . value. Our . . . values stay the same from year to year but what changes is the mentor we learn about and their stories. So, for example, [for the value of] Optimism [we chose] Misty Copeland. We chose that term for her because part of her story is not having the ballerina body type and phenotype but still persevering and showing that [if] you have your skill, your confidence, you will get to your goal." These values are woven into the school day, as students are asked by teachers: "What is the . . . value? Who are the [womanist women] that represent it, and how do they show it?" In the morning, teachers discuss with the students how they use that value at home or outside of school. Throughout the week, staff members keep track of different acts that display values and give rewards at the end of the week to the girls who embodied the values the most.

Introducing powerful, inspirational women along with the values is critical. "I think it's allowing students to have a mirror,"

Principal Knight states. "And it's good to hear that people can struggle but they always come out stronger on the other end. The women we are picking are multicultural . . . [for example] she was a soul-cycle instructor and now she is an Adidas ambassador and she tried out 30 times! Next year, we are trying to pick more girls in our community . . . I think the ability to make connections to these women drives the students to be awesome human beings."

Teachers use these dynamic women role models to educate their students about strength and overcoming challenges.[44] For example, during my visit to Teele Elementary, students were taught about singer, actress, and civil rights activist Lena Horne, who was the first African American woman to sign a long-term contract with a major studio. Students, when asked to document why she inspired them, provided the following responses:

> Lena Horne inspires me because she reached to her goal and became a famous singer and actress. Even though she was a Black woman and couldn't perform with White people, she still took action in her dream and was able to inspire many people in the world.

> Lena Horne inspires me because she shows me that if I work hard enough I could achieve my dreams just like her and become a great success in life.

> She left home just to support her family and she became a dancer and became known as one of the top African American performers of her time, and she did her work with civil rights group, refused to play roles that stereotyped African American women.

The students' responses reflect how learning about these role models teaches them important lessons not only about hard work and persistence but also about the barriers associated with being a woman of color in the United States. As one teacher remarked on the effects of the curriculum, "It really opens their minds to different things that can be a barrier to girls in different ways." Through their exposure to these barriers, students also learn that, just like the women they read about, they can have myriad challenges in their lives and still become successful individuals. Most important, the success they are being exposed to extends beyond academics.

Beyond historically notable women who have overcome obstacles to find success, the curriculum also highlights contemporary heroes who are women, most notably the founders of the Black Lives Matter movement: Alicia Garza, Patrisse Cullors, and Opal Tometi. During the year of my study, students were taught about these women and the founding principles of the movement that was created in response to police violence against African Americans in the United States. In addition, an assignment was created around exploring activism and why the founding women were womanist women. Fourth-grade girls were asked to describe how they were inspired to make a change in the world and what impact they believed the movement had on their future. Responses to the former question included the following:

> Because they inspire me to do anything I want to. Because they believed that racial profiling was wrong and created the whole movement #Blacklivesmatter. So, if they can do that, I can be a lawyer, a teacher, an astronaut, the president, because they taught me anything I put my mind to can happen.
>
> I should fight for something that is unfair, something that I disagree with.

Because they went above and beyond, instead of just resting . . . so Blacks and Hispanics can get the treatment they deserve. And since only three Black women did it by themselves, it tells me that they had to work really hard to get the movement in motion.

These females make me believe that everyone needs the opportunity to have their voice be heard. Especially girls and girls of color.

When asked about their expectations of the impact it would have on their future, the students responded with the following:

I will not tolerate anyone being racist to another person in front of me because the racist problem will gain more throughout the world and then people of color will feel [that they don't belong] and sad and that they don't matter. So in the future, everyone should know that they're special in many ways!

In the future, Blacks are going to be treated more fairly.

Being a young Black woman, I might not be who people want me to be, but this movement shows, no matter how much hate I get because of my skin color, I know that I matter so that's all that matters. Even [though] I may be different from the world, I know that these women gave me the right to speak my mind and [that] I matter and so do you.

These responses reveal not only a sophisticated understanding of what the movement seeks to achieve but also hope that it may contribute to a better world. Students are taught to acknowledge race and gender inequality but also to recognize the steps that are being taken by others to address inequality. They are being educated on these issues and empowered to believe they can help address them. As stated by Principal Knight: "A lot of things are influenced by the stories they hear . . . they don't just want to be lawyers. They say things like, 'I want to be a cheerleader for Black people.'" In several cases, students take a specific stand on the role they intend to play in improving a problem, such as not tolerating "anyone being racist to another person." The lessons learned play a crucial role in building self-belief and self-efficacy, critical skills for developing achievement-oriented identities, and exemplify a feminist practice of teaching students to speak out against injustices and believing in their ability to transgress them.

As part of the discussion of the Black Lives Matter movement, students were also given room to express their feelings toward the victims of police killings, particularly Rekia Boyd and Tamir Rice, who were close to their age when they died. Through letters written to the victims, students shared their empathy: "I know this letter will never reach you, but I wanted to say this was really unfair. It was just a toy or [N]erf gun or a water gun. You did not do anything wrong, you're innocent! And the police did not get charged."

They also share their fears and wishes: "This means a lot to me because I have 12 toy guns, and me and my friends play with them every day. Let God bless you, and I hope you made it to heaven."

Additionally, they provide them with affirmation: "Don't regret being Black. Love your race and be proud of who you are," and "Even though you died, you're strong. You're still strong and you will always be strong."

Finally, they assure them that people are fighting on their behalf: "I am here to say there is good news, people are protesting and trying to stand up for the people who were shot for no reason. Now you won't have to feel bad. People care for you as a Black person so be proud that you have brothers and sisters standing up for you." The exercise is sad but necessary. It enables students to develop mechanisms to cope with the events they see on their televisions, cell phones, and computers every day. From these lessons, students build the identities necessary to confront the hard truths of being a Black youth in today's America.

Looking to the Future

Teele Elementary stands out, first and foremost, as an institution that protects its students and impresses upon them the need for positive, or rather, achievement-oriented identities. These identities are built through the school's efforts to dismantle the gender barriers faced by girls and to provide them with the confidence and strategies necessary to transgress challenges inhibiting their net achievement. In doing so, the school serves as a close model for gender equity: it approximates a feminist institution that helps girls thrive.[45]

What happens when these girls leave Teele Elementary after the fourth grade? The statistics are not in their favor. While more Black women and girls in the United States attend and graduate secondary educational institutions than ever before, they may also be subject to high rates of suspension, expulsion, and entry into juvenile justice centers.[46] When Black women graduate from high school, research demonstrates that they are more than twice as likely as all other groups to attend for-profit colleges, many of which lack accreditation and use predatory financial practices.[47] The consequence is that these young women take on loans they cannot afford to repay to earn degrees that are unlikely to land them well-paying jobs.[48]

Once in the job market, Black women not only struggle to land well-paying jobs, but also suffer from higher levels of unemployment, even though they are the group most likely to be a single head of household.[49] As expectant mothers, Black women are twice as likely as expectant White mothers to experience the death of their infant. These disparities persist even among expectant Black mothers with an advanced degree.[50] Regarding death, Black women are also twice as likely as White women to die from homicides, in large part due to the violence of an intimate partner.[51] Altogether, Black women and girls face myriad struggles over the course of their lifetimes that inevitably impact their ability to thrive.

We don't know if students at Teele Elementary will retain their lessons about gender, race, confidence, and transgression. Will they make a difference, especially once they enter much more hostile environments? The administration at Teele Elementary knows that outcomes are uncertain. As one teacher put it, "I just hope they retain their confidence." Her goals for them are in no way modest.

While it is unclear whether these girls will be able to hold on to the skills they gain at Teele Elementary, they have developed a foundation from which much can be built. In particular, Teele Elementary disrupts dominant power relations and helps students grow to feel confident in their voice and thus secure in speaking up and taking up space. They also create curricula that teach students not only about how to recognize race and gender inequality but also how to transgress it by taking on these issues at school and within their communities. Finally, Teele Elementary encourages dialogue around physical appearance and standards of beauty, thereby enabling girls to defy stereotypes and rebuild more positive identities.

With this feminist school foundation, girls at Teele gain a tool kit that can be put to use as they grow and develop. Of course, this tool kit does not relieve society from its moral responsibility to be equitable, but it does engender pragmatic hope for girls while we wait. Sadly, that is much more than is provided to most poor girls of color in the United States.

Becoming
Achievement Oriented

No matter what anybody says, we can't have it all.
Not if you are a woman. Not yet.

—AMA ATA AIDOO

FOR DECADES, Academy Prep Secondary School (APSS) was considered the school of last resort.[1]

Kwame Owusu, the assistant headmaster of APSS, explained the challenges his school was facing when I arrived in Ghana in 2009. "Being surrounded by some settlements . . . the squatters, they pose difficulty for us . . . they open liquor shops, sell drugs. [APSS] is more or less a community school . . . and we are [also] a day school so those who cannot afford a boarding school send their kids to us." When I asked the students about their perceptions of the school, a girl named Ama exclaimed, "This is [APSS], the most stubborn school in Ghana, the most notorious, the most indisciplined." Another girl, Lydia, interrupted to point out the additional burden of being a girl at APSS: "girls drop out because of pregnancies and other things." In describing the school as "stubborn," "notorious," and a place where girls drop out, the students explained why APSS came to be known as the option for "those who cannot afford a boarding school."

That is, until Mary Mensah arrived.

In 2007, Mary Mensah became the first woman to head APSS in its sixty-year history. When I met her in 2009, she was not only the first woman to head the school but also the only woman in its senior administration.

Born into a middle-class home, Mary Mensah is the oldest of three children. While her siblings moved to the United States and Europe to pursue their careers, she remained in Ghana and rose through the educational ranks. Her experience moving up the ranks has sensitized her to the challenges that girls face at APSS.

Like many schools in Ghana, APSS only began accepting girl students in 1990. Although the school's acceptance of girls indicates a country seeking change in a positive direction, girl students have struggled to adjust to the school setting. As Mary said the first day we spoke: "Now what I notice about the females in this school . . . the girls in the school, they tend to be a bit timid. I think it has to do with their cultural background."

Mary speaks slowly and confidently. She punctuates every few phrases with a flash of her pristine smile. She continued, "But I have a different background where the male and female are given the same opportunities, so I try to bring this to bear on my leadership." In talking about the girls at the school, Mary touched on the sociocultural context in which most girls and women find themselves: an environment that in more than one way favors boys and men. In contrast, Mary viewed her household as providing equal opportunities for both the men and women in her family. Accordingly, Mary became intent on creating a similarly equal environment at APSS. Her efforts to increase girls' enrollment have paid off: as of 2017, girls made up nearly 50 percent of all students enrolled in APSS.

Ama is one of those girls. When I met her in 2009, she lived with her mother, grandmother, and two siblings in a one-room shack. She was in her third year at APSS and had ambitions to be the first in her family to go to college. Yet, being from a poor family, her ambitions were met with resistance by her mother and her surrounding community.

"When you get ready to go to school and they see you moving in your uniform, they tend to laugh at you," Ama said, describing the reactions she received on her agonizing walk to school every morning.

Ama's agony was exacerbated by her mother. On the topic of school, she told Ama, "You won't be able to make it. You can't even get through [junior high school] or [senior high school]. How much more for college?"

Ama responded, "Mom, I will. You watch." Ama told me that she thought about her mother's disapproval in the following way: "I see it as a challenge. She is throwing a challenge at me, and I am throwing one back to show her that I can be better than she thinks I am."

Not many young people who experience direct resistance to their ambitions from both their community and their family would be able to respond in that way.[2] But to my surprise, many girls I met at APSS do. I wanted to know who these girls were. Would they make it to college? And, if so, how? More important, where did they get this can-do attitude? Was it formed in school, or by the influence of a role model? And finally, do their can-do attitudes last?

The Importance of Grit and Perseverance in Developing Countries

Education studies emphasize the significant role of noncognitive skills such as grit and perseverance in the success of students. While the budding research on these so-called soft skills has produced promising evidence about the crucial role they may play, the verdict is still out on whether people are born with them or if they can be taught. It is thought that if educators can find ways to teach soft skills *and* make them stick, students might succeed even if they come from environments where such skills are not fostered.

Earlier studies suggested that students were more likely to demonstrate noncognitive skills if schools such as APSS created environments which facilitated their development.[3] Very little of this work has explored how gender affects noncognitive skills and educational achievement, or even what the relationship is between these soft skills and academic performance in Ghana and other so-called developing societies.[4] In a study on noncognitive skills and academic performance conducted in 2010, George Frempong, a policy researcher, found that confidence levels rather than the location or quality of the school explained the disparate academic outcomes of students from low- and high-education backgrounds in Ghana. He found these results to be especially strong among the girl students sampled, which reinforces the notion that confidence, a noncognitive skill, is more critical for academic achievement than factors typically studied, such as parental education level and school quality.[5] The findings indicate that the teaching of noncognitive skills to girls might help reduce disparities in academic outcomes across Ghana, but virtually no studies in Ghana investigate this claim. Furthermore, by focusing only on the relationship between noncognitive skills and academic performance, the study's results are based on relatively narrow evaluations of achievement.

Margaret Frye's research on school-aged girls in Malawi examines the role of educational institutions, development organizations, and the media in espousing an ideological rhetoric of a "brighter future" to promote the value of girls' education. She finds that this rhetoric encourages an inflated sense of girls' chances of educational achievement and life success in light of the disadvantages girl students face. Frye explains this disconnect as attributable to the fact that girls in Malawi learn to evaluate themselves based on their ability to be virtuous women—of high moral standard. Girls' perceptions of themselves as virtuous contribute to their confidence and positive attitudes toward learning, or as I would say, their net achievement.[6]

While developing confidence and positive attitudes toward learning are clearly positive outcomes, Frye's findings also point to the danger of building educational identities on rhetoric espoused by external bodies rather than delivered by the school itself. More specifically, she highlights how claims to virtue, rather than an inherent belief that girls are deserving, has become the predominant reason to pursue education among girls already marginalized within society.

Frempong's and Frye's studies emphasize the potential role of noncognitive skills in evaluations of academic performance and net achievement across different contexts. I argue, however, that most literature on noncognitive skills does not address how these skills are used to combat the gender-based barriers, such as sexual harassment, which girls face in their everyday educational environments. Unlike noncognitive skills, the concept of achievement-oriented identities (AOIs) requires, first, that educators understand the specific inhibitors girls face. Second, this concept requires a focused effort among teachers and administrators to develop girls' self-efficacy and confidence before providing them with specific tools to strategically respond to challenges and transgress norms at school and in the world. In short, AOIs are the tools feminist schools provide students to effect change in society and reach their individual goals.

Achievement-Oriented Identities

In this chapter I document why schools should facilitate the development of achievement-oriented identities as a more comprehensive approach to teaching noncognitive skills. The term *AOIs* can be used to describe positive beliefs in one's own ability, and the facility to translate those beliefs into realizable actions through the development of confidence, strategy, and transgression. AOIs constitute a tool kit that helps girls think and respond in proactive ways to the challenges before them. These identities are constantly being shaped and reinforced by all aspects of a school's culture, whether by the school's leadership or in the classroom.

Accordingly, I explain how AOIs orient a school's institutional culture toward net achievement, which impresses upon students a positive academic identity. Evidence of the context AOIs provide schools can be observed through the intentional actions of teachers and school leaders, in addition to the activities conducted throughout the typical school day. The context's influence on its students can be observed through the goals students express and the proactive strategies they take in response to challenges at school and in the world.

Education in Ghana

Despite its progressive education policies, Ghana continues to experience disparities in educational outcomes for its youth. In 1957, Ghana became the first African country south of the Sahara to gain independence from British colonial rule. Shortly after, in 1961, Ghana became the first African nation to provide universal education under its Education Act. This effort, while progressive in theory, was unfortunately unrealized in practice. Despite the promise of free education for all, the nation faced multiple political and financial challenges. Thus, a number of identifiable groups found themselves excluded from the educational system.[7] When the new republic was established in 1992, however, an equal rights amendment was included in the constitution, establishing what came to be known as Free and Compulsory Universal Basic Education (FCUBE). It was only then that the number of girls attending school began to increase significantly. These domestic policies—in tandem with a number of international policies, such as those included in the Millennium Development Goals (MDGs) and the Convention on the Elimination of All Forms of Discrimination Against Women (CEDAW), in addition to the development of local government agencies such as the Ministry of Women and Children's Affairs (MOWAC)—have created space for what seems to be changing societal perspectives on women in Ghana.

In 2008, the speaker of the parliament of Ghana was a woman, as was the chief justice and the attorney general. In 2011, Samia Nkrumah became the first woman to head a major political party, and, in 2012, three vice-presidential candidates were women. Descriptive representation aside, local civil society dedicated to women has made huge strides, including the development of the Women's Manifesto for Ghana in 2004—a comprehensive list of demands to political parties; the passage of the nation's first domestic violence act in 2007; and, in 2012, the development of a national gender policy.

With regard to education today, Ghana boasts near gender parity (.96 on the Gender Parity Index) at the primary level with over 90 percent of the country's population attaining at least basic education. Yet as the education levels rise, there are significant drops in enrollment, particularly among girl students from disadvantaged socioeconomic backgrounds.[8] Financial means and gendered responsibilities play significant roles in the ability of girl students to pass into higher levels of education.

Public schools are technically free, but schools often charge students fees for services including registration, books, and supplies. These fees make even government-subsidized schools still relatively unaffordable for some.[9] These fees typically increase at higher levels of education, which can impact how many girls, especially, are able to stay in school.

Even once girls gain access to schools, they may have trouble remaining enrolled. Girls may face challenges boys do not. For example, girls often bear more responsibility at home compared with their male peers. They may walk several miles to fetch water for their family before school or do hours of housework after school. For this reason, when parents are faced with financial hardship and must choose which of their children should stay in school, they consider boys over their girl siblings. These gendered decisions further disadvantage girls' prospects for educational success.

Within the classroom, girls face challenges unique to their gender as well. For example, in selecting an academic track for students, many teachers in Ghana still hold outdated views about girl students' capacity to perform in certain disciplines. Consequently, girl students are funneled into the arts or home sciences even if they have the aptitude and interest to pursue traditionally male-dominated subjects such as math and science.[10] A lack of interest in their assigned academic track can lead girl students to lose interest in school altogether.

Another more recent concern is that of male teachers and administrators pursuing sexual relationships with girl students. More specifically, girls must contend with what one expert I interviewed called "STGs," or "sexually transmitted grades." She used the term to describe the process by which a girl student is asked for a sexual favor in exchange for accurate reporting of her academic work. So even though more girls are attending higher levels of school, they are also facing increasing sexual harassment in the classroom. This problem is exacerbated by the fact that teachers are predominantly male, and in Ghana, girls are often afraid to speak out against male authority figures for fear of retaliation.[11]

Thus, despite recent developments in public policy, girls in Ghana continue to operate under the context of patriarchal hierarchies and traditional gender norms.[12] The potential for a girl to achieve in Ghana is related not only to gaining educational access but also to developing the capacity to navigate everyday societal barriers based on gender, a dilemma that can be resolved if girls' achievement-oriented identities are recognized and fostered.

Achievement for Girls at APSS

This chapter uses original data collected between 2009 and 2012 on the educational experiences of girls attending APSS in Ghana to demonstrate how the school shaped attitudes critical for girls to develop achievement-oriented identities. APSS is a four-year government-subsidized school founded in 1946 and made public in 1954. It long acted as a neighborhood school for the kids of Coco Bay until it moved about thirteen miles east to its current location in 1987. While its proximity to Coco Bay is originally what attracted families in that neighborhood to APSS, many still attended even after the move.

At the time of my study, APSS had more than 1,000 students and a gender ratio of sixty girls to forty boys. More than 80 percent of its students lived within a ten- to fifteen-mile radius of the campus, and nearly 75 percent came from low-income backgrounds, defined in Ghana as earning 2 USD or less per day (or between 100 and 350 Ghanian cedis per month.[13]

A product of its environment, APSS is a microcosm for gender relations in Ghana at large; it has experienced a lot of progress and some setbacks. Accordingly, most girls who attend APSS face the same burdens as Ama: They are both beneficiaries as well as victims of the educate-the-girl-child policies meant to help them.

While the opportunity to attend school is potentially life changing, girls in Ghana often come from neighborhoods and households that rebuke their decision, and they attend schools that have few resources and are far from practicing gender equality. Still, these girls are expected to achieve and have the desire to achieve as well. Unless they have unwavering resilience or are academically exceptional, however, these students may never meet that expectation. I returned to Ghana, and APSS, for several years after the completion of the study to see what these girls had achieved.

During the active years of the study, I observed Headmistress Mary as she assessed the larger issues of patriarchy and gender inequality and their effects on girl students. She designed solutions that the school could use to help the girls be less timid, have more self-belief, and respond to the gender-based challenges they regularly experienced at school and at home. These actions took place across the institution—at the senior leadership level through changes in policy, after school through clubs and activities, and within the classroom through the addition of religion and moral education courses.[14]

The Role of Women Leaders

In the effort to improve net achievement for girls, school leadership matters. And in Ghana, this is no different. From Day One, Headmistress Mary's approach to leadership, especially in relation to her girl students, became a critical element to any success they ultimately achieved. Mary viewed her identification as a woman as opportune for engaging in discussions and activities around gender: "Since I am female, it has given me an opportunity to mold the females in the school. I try to encourage them . . . make them feel like there is nothing like you being an inferior sex."

During my time at APSS, I witnessed Mary's actions align with her professed desires as she made several deliberate decisions to redirect the girls at the school. For example, inside and outside of her office, Mary posted motivational sayings and messages weekly. One, for example, read, "Be a woman with attitude and a lady with class." In her office stood a mug that she showed to each girl, including myself. It read, "Act like a lady, think like a man, and work like a dog." These clearly gendered messages reflected Mary's views on the values she sought to instill in her girl students. Mary described herself as needing to share these messages because she is "the only female, the school is now 65 years, and it's been headed by males."

Indeed, her messages also raise questions about respectability, or rather what it means to be "a lady with class," yet students appeared to internalize these messages and empathize with them, given their responses to the headmistress's actions. As one girl student stated, "If you are a woman, and you're in that position . . . men hate to see women in that position, so she has to be that way . . . so in working hours she has a tough face but after that she is sweet." This student understands the gendered dimensions associated with the headmistress's role as both a woman and an administrator. Her words also reflect a clear subscription to the rhetoric being promoted around campus. Headmistress Mary's presence as a woman in a male-dominated space mattered.

Doing What Boys Do

At APSS girls faced the practical issue of being underrepresented across all classrooms, but especially within the science, technology, engineering, and mathematics (STEM) academic track. When girls were first asked in 2009 about the disparities existing between the genders, one student responded, "The boys, I don't know they just do better . . . I don't know why . . . you do the same thing as they are doing but you work harder." Another girl student complained that she found the presence of boys in her class to be distracting: "Sometimes when you want to learn is when they begin to make noise. I try to explain to them we are here for something but they don't get it that way."

These experiences affect girls' perceptions of their ability to compete with boys. One of the best-performing students at the school, Lydia, states, "It's a perception that we girls have . . . we can do something but we can't be the best . . . even if we are going for it, we can't really match up to the guys, and I think it has to be erased, it needs to be eliminated." Lydia's statement reflects the headmistress's hope that girls' negative perceptions of their skills can be changed.

Perhaps of the most obvious indicator of Headmistress Mary's goals was her decision to encourage Lydia to be the girls' prefect during the first year of my study, 2009. Despite her professed confidence when I spoke to Lydia in the second year of the study, in 2010, Lydia admitted that when she was asked to be prefect she did not want to participate because she was told not to get involved in leadership roles. More specifically, she states: "At first I did not believe in myself. From the house, I wasn't being encouraged. I remember even before I came to [APSS], they were telling me don't get into any leadership roles. 'It will be too stressful for you.'"

Lydia, like Ama, also aspired to be the first girl in her family to go to college. She was raised by her mother, who worked full time as house help for a wealthy family. Her father died when she was twelve years old. Since he was the main breadwinner of the family, after his death Lydia was sent to live with an aunt, who agreed to cover her high school fees if Lydia agreed to clean her house and care for her shop. The arrangement proved to be difficult in more ways than one. Most relevant, her aunt did not support her educational aspirations and discouraged Lydia from taking on leadership roles and applying to college.

Yet with the encouragement of Headmistress Mary, Lydia applied for the prefect position anyway. In 2010, she became the head girls' prefect of the school. That same year, the headmistress changed the policy around the annual speech and prize-giving day. Defying tradition, she appointed the girls' prefect to give the keynote speech, rather than the boys' prefect. Through her actions, Mary not only challenged Lydia to speak before a crowd, but also challenged others' expectations of who should be able to speak. Her actions encouraged Lydia to evolve from timid student to self-confident speaker. As she states: "I was so nervous. All this time I said to myself, no one else is going to do it. You have to do it. So let's just get it done and do it all right."

Reflecting on the impact of the speech a year later, Headmistress Mary explained, "Today [Lydia] can stand in front of the school and give a speech without winking. That shows what the female leadership of this school has done." And indeed, referring directly to the experience of giving the speech, Lydia exclaims, "After I was done, I had so much confidence, I felt like I could do anything . . . like there is nothing I can't do."

In response to the question of how competitive girls are compared with boys at the school, Headmistress Mary stated, "Now you can look around and see that the girls rub shoulders with the guys . . . This confidence has grown to the extent that students are really excited whenever you throw a challenge to them." A similar sentiment is shared by the assistant headmaster as he recounts the story of Lydia and others: "Our girls have done well . . . They are rubbing shoulders with the boys." In a separate interview, Lydia affirms these comments with the following statement: "I compete with them and I beat them . . . [chuckles] well not necessarily 'beat,' but I perform better than they do."

Altogether, Lydia's story shows how the actions of a school, and its school leadership, can have a dramatic impact on girl students' self-confidence and attitudes toward learning. Indeed, by encouraging Lydia to apply for a leadership role (despite being discouraged from doing so at home), allowing her to give the keynote (despite it being inconsistent with custom and tradition), and coaching her to bring out her voice (despite her clear nervousness), APSS—under the auspices of Headmistress Mary—taught Lydia to be confident and strategic, and to transgress norms both at home and at school. Mary's attentiveness to the tactics employed and the calculated consequences of her strategies are important in understanding how achievement-oriented identities developed among her students thereafter.

Practicing Student Leadership

After-school activities, such as student government, facilitate connections between students and act as additional mechanisms for reinforcing AOIs. These activities also provide leadership opportunities for girl students not found in other areas of their lives. For many years at APSS, the representation of girls in student executive leadership roles was low. Fortunately, during the second year of my study, Ama became the first girl vice president of the student government in sixty-two years. Unfortunately, however, Ama became vice president during a period when the school was especially pinched for resources. In her role she led a successful campaign to raise funds for the purchase of fifty new chairs so that "students could have a place to sit and learn." While Ama described the role as difficult, stating that, "people expect you to speak when everyone's mouth is quiet," the opportunity to participate in student government, particularly in an executive leadership position, gave Ama the confidence to raise her concerns and find a way to get them addressed. Ama described the student government members as being "proud of ourselves . . . to be the first group to give something back to the school."

Ama also discovered that her role gave her the confidence and strategic skills to take on even more serious gender issues at the school: "A teacher was molesting one of the girl students. I got close to him, [but] he did not know that I was stabbing him in the back. I got together with my executives, and we reported the teacher. The next thing we know, he put in his resignation notice to leave the school before he got to know it was me." When asked how she had the courage to report the incident, Ama described herself as "not afraid of anything," and went on to state, "I have seen all that I have to see. I don't think I am afraid to face anyone or anything . . . I don't want to be like everyone, I want to prove a point that there still can be someone good from the Zungo [low income slum] where no one thinks there can be. That's what I want to do: I want to prove a point."

Ama's leadership role in student government clearly provided a mechanism for her to translate the courage she derives from her neighborhood environment into a successful campaign to end sexual violence in the school. Yet Ama's actions are undoubtedly conditional on being able to safely report the incident of sexual harassment to the school's administration, without fear of retaliation. Accordingly, the lessons taught and opportunities available through these after-school activities—from raising school funds to taking action against a predator and holding him accountable—play an important role in encouraging girl students to have confidence in their abilities to strategically transgress the gender biases institutionalized at their school.

Perhaps the value of AOIs absorbed by Ama at school, and its persistence in other contexts, is even more telling in her response to the discouragement she continually heard from her mother: "When I [hear] my mother say, 'You will not be able to finish [senior high school], you will not be able to go to a university,' I say 'Mom, you are wrong. I will be able to finish [senior high school], I will go to a university, I will work. It's like, sit down [and] look at me.'"

In her last year at APSS, Ama worked part time to afford college applications. When she first applied to college after graduation, she was denied admission. She applied again the following year and was admitted into one of Ghana's top universities. Ama's experience with successfully taking on challenges in her leadership role in student government, the affirmation she received by being selected to be vice president, and the responsiveness from school leadership to her courageous decision to stand against sexual assault likely moderated the lack of affirmation received from her mother. Ama's can-do attitude likely played an important role in her decision to apply to college a second time, even after being rejected. Together, these skills—confidence, strategy, and transgression—culminate in a set of skills critical for working toward her personal academic goals, despite her doubly disadvantaged background as a low-income young woman.

How Girls Are Taught Matters

During my time at APSS I found that the school's emphasis on religious and moral education contributed to the belief that girl students could succeed despite the barriers before them. The creation of formal institutions of education across Ghana was largely the work of colonial Christian missionaries decades ago.[15] Many of the religious activities rooted in traditional Christian schools, such as morning worship, have been institutionalized in educational practices in Ghana through the present day. For example, most government-subsidized schools continue to teach religion and moral education courses at the basic, junior, and secondary school levels. These courses and related activities promote positive messaging around "belief" and "overcoming" and encourage students to hold these perceptions. In particular, the religious and moral education courses emphasize the importance of spirituality, specifically faith in God, for overcoming education barriers and achieving future aspirations. Consequently, the existence of these religious and spiritual activities works to reinforce components of the achievement-oriented framework.

For example, every morning assembly at APSS is opened with prayer. A typical prayer said at these assemblies might be: "Dear Lord, we thank you for bringing us here safely. It wasn't for our strength. It wasn't for our might. It wasn't for our energy. You delivered us out of the hands of the evil one. Amen."

In addition, motivational sayings posted on bulletin boards throughout the campus have a religious or spiritual message:

> Success keeps you glowing, but only God keeps you going.
> Let us thank the Lord for making us feel so beautiful for ourselves and for each other.
> When the prophetic grace is poured on you, even your mistakes will become ladders to your success.

As displayed, the school's strategic use of these messages enables them to connect religious values such as "grace" to academic "success" for students. And certainly, it appears that those values are translated to the students. When a girl student was asked in 2010, "What does it take to be academically successful?" she responded, "In order to be successful, you have to be determined, just believe in yourself, you have to know who you are . . . you have to know those abilities . . . those talents that God has deposited in you . . . so that you can unearth them for the benefit of yourself and the benefit of the whole nation."

This student is connecting her academic abilities and future aspirations to her belief in God. Statements that directly invoked God were common across all students examined. A clear example of the role of religion in shaping educational aspirations is highlighted in this response from Lydia in 2011 to the question of how she would be able to afford college: "I have a faith that . . .

God is going to make a way. I figured out thinking and worrying won't solve any problem, so I just have to pray to God." From this response, it appears that religion and spirituality are contributing to the construction of Lydia's worldview. Accordingly, even if a student does not regularly attend church or identify in a strong way with a religion, the pervasiveness of religious messages still structures critical aspects of her educational experience.

Although religious messages can be used in negative ways, in Lydia's case they contributed specifically to her development of self-efficacy. Schools draw on religious and spiritual accepted wisdom to instill educational values of self-efficacy in large part because girls have already learned how to strategically maneuver and transgress prescribed gender confines. Their ability to consciously navigate gender confines enables them to take on the aspects of religion that are most beneficial. Ultimately, then, development of girls' self-efficacy, in this case through religious messages, acts as a critical base on which their achievement-oriented identities are built. These religious messages also likely play an important role in girls' persistence in the face of difficult odds.

The Persistence of Achievement-Oriented Identities after Secondary School

Once Lydia graduated, she took a break from school in order to work and save money to apply to college. A year later, in 2012, she was admitted into a top school in Ghana but could not afford to enroll. When I asked her how she felt about it, she responded: "You have some of your colleagues in school . . . they call you [and say] oh this and this is happening . . . and you feel so bad because you haven't been able and you're still not too sure you will be going to school and you feel anxious. So I was trying to check on my application for the scholarship but nothing was happening. I was trying to look for other alternatives . . . other things I can do."

I then asked her the same question I had asked her the year before, "Do you see any barriers to achieving the goals you have set for yourself?" Lydia responded, "I know next year someone will have to pay; I cannot say I am afraid of that. I don't have fear because I have faith." Even a year after graduating, Lydia continued to profess a strong belief in her ability to find a way that is clearly influenced by her faith. Her experiences at APSS reinforced her belief.

In 2012, I also asked Headmistress Mary about Lydia and the challenges she was experiencing. She responded by stating, "Here was a brilliant student and a girl as such . . . I told [her] you will go to school no matter what." Both Lydia and the headmistress showed a similarly high level of confidence in Lydia's ability to be successful in overcoming her challenges, even though objectively she did not have the resources to do so.

Ama, like Lydia, also did not have the resources but got into college. When I asked her in 2012 if she was excited for college, she responded: "I am not that excited because I am going to school without the gadgets that I need. So psychologically I am down . . . I have to just sort it out. But what really encourages me [is that] I am the only female from my mom and dad's side . . . the first girl to go to college." Ama is keenly aware of her disadvantaged social and economic position. She is equally aware of why it is important for her to move forward regardless as "the first girl to go to college." Students like her, who objectively appear to have none of the factors traditionally associated with academic achievement in terms of resources or parental support, highlight how noncognitive skills such as confidence, strategic skills, and the ability to transgress might contribute to their ultimate net achievement. The school, especially through its leadership, curriculum, after-school activities, and peer networks, helps students develop these qualities and retain them after they have left secondary school.

Not all the students examined had the same outcomes. Some went straight to college ($n = 4$) instead of waiting an entire year ($n = 4$). Others waited more than a year ($n = 3$), one joined the army ($n = 1$), and several changed their goals from traditional college to teacher training schools ($n = 5$). Nonetheless, the positive identities shaped at the school appeared to remain relatively intact. Statements by these former APSS students, such as "When I say I'm doing something, I have to get to the highest point," and "I am focused, I know what I am about, and I know what I am here for" indicate the persistence of achievement-oriented thinking.

By the time these APSS students graduate, they have acquired important values that will serve them throughout their lives. Most important, they have developed a belief that they have acquired the necessary skills to meet challenges—to be confident, strategic, and transgressive in handling a hostile society. Achievement-oriented identities are about developing the tools to react and engage when faced with obstacles in the world. This is what the school context has impressed upon these students.

The labor of dealing with educational inequality should rest with the school. School, of course, cannot fully protect its students. Students should not have to deal with issues such as sexual harassment, in or out of school. The conditions for success should not require girls to be resilient or to engage in additional labor to dismantle inequality. But in the real world, these inequalities persist. If we accept the premise that educational inequality should be properly addressed by the school, then it is the work of the school to create conditions for girls to thrive. Thriving in a hostile society involves not only having an equitable school to attend but also acquiring the tools to navigate an inequitable society. If schools foster an environment in which students are encouraged to build such a tool kit, then schools are developing student identities oriented toward achievement.

The Value of College for Girls in Ghana

It's obvious that in Ghana it is a significant achievement for girl students to graduate from secondary school and to be accepted into college. Still, when I present my research at American institutions, I often get asked, "How many of these girls who make it to college—if they graduate—will actually get a job?" The truth is, many probably will not. This is a country that continues to struggle with high levels of unemployment, and young women often get the short end of the stick. Nonetheless, a degree certainly improves their odds of employment.

However, the question brings to the light the differences in how college is perceived in the United States and Ghana. In the United States, students go to college as the first step toward a career. In fact, it is nearly impossible in the United States today to earn a livable wage without a two- or four-year college degree. In recent years, as more US students have graduated and have been unable to find meaningful careers, especially jobs that match their skills or are in their intended career path, major discussions have arisen about the utility of higher education altogether. Even though higher education has acted as a path toward gender equality in the United States, structural inequities in the workplace, from the invisible glass ceiling to pay inequities in salaries, have been obstacles for women in the corporate world. The obdurate nature of these obstacles raises questions about whether the success women have experienced in the United States is equivalent with its intent.

In Sub-Saharan African countries like Ghana, the utility of going to college, particularly for girls, is often framed differently. At the societal level, educated women are more likely to immunize their children, less likely to contract HIV, and more likely to reinvest in their family's education. Their children are more likely to survive past the age of five, and more likely as well to get married and have children later.[16] The societal benefits, therefore, also play an important role in making a case for the value of attending college that extends far beyond getting a job. At the individual level, college is seen as a mechanism of social mobility. Many factors make college an attractive option for girls. They meet many new people, learn how to live independently, and become more highly respected in their communities.

The experience of college graduates in Ghana stands out because the country has a long-standing national service program in which college students are required to work for the government for one full year within two years of graduation. The students are offered a very modest monthly stipend for food and transportation. The experience helps them gain skills and develop connections with potential employers. While there are a lot of challenges with the program related to finding quality positions to fit graduates' interests and skill sets, the program assures girls and their families that if they graduate, they are guaranteed employment for at least one year after college. This type of program is crucial particularly for girls because upon graduating from college, girls are expected to either contribute to the household or get married and start a family. This program buys girls time to figure out how to find a job and reintegrate into a social context that is often much less progressive than their college environment.

When these girls come home, especially as the first in their families to go to college, they have a high level of confidence in their abilities and pride in what they have accomplished. They are often able to convince their families of the power of education simply through the symbolic prestige it affords them. Thus, the act of going to college becomes a powerful tool not only because of their potential ability to get a job but also because of the many personal, symbolic, and social benefits associated with the degree.

Self-Delusion or Self-Belief?

To be sure, there were many times during my research when I heard girl students express such a high level of optimism in their ability to attend college that I worried they were not being realistic. On one hand, I enjoyed the departure from the rather hopeless perspectives I often heard from students living in low-income neighborhoods in other contexts I studied. On the other hand, I feared their self-belief may have been veering toward self-delusion.

The girl students I worked with were by all measures objectively poor. Many of their parents worked as petty traders, lacked formal education, and resided in Ghana's poorest urban slums. Furthermore, whatever school the girls happened to attend was not necessarily a pipeline to college. In fact, only 20 percent of Ghana's high schools provide 80 percent of the nation's college students. The 20 percent are often legacy schools of colonial Ghana that serve the country's economic elite. In short, these schools were not the type of institutions that the poor students I worked with typically attended.

The clear disparity between the ambitions of these girls and the objective reality raises questions about the value of this growth mindset. What is the value of grit if you are objectively poor? What does it mean to work hard and be accepted into college but not have the resources to attend? Is it useful to encourage students to believe they can go to college when the odds are so clearly stacked against them?

The answer to this last question is mostly "yes." Indeed, believing in their own abilities should positively contribute to their outcomes. To be sure, many of them will still fall short of achieving these goals, but the pursuit heightens the probability that they may be successful. For example, I saw girls fail their college entrance exams and retake them multiple times. I witnessed them work for multiple years to save money, and I even saw them borrow money to pay for college applications and work a part-time job to pay it off. I witnessed girls continue to make a way out of no way, just to be the first girl in their family to go to college.

Nonetheless, while the girls described in this chapter fit neatly into common conceptions of resilience and individual agency, their actual entry and success in college was made possible by the schools they attended and the people around them. Consider Lydia, who came from a single-parent home and a very poor background. She was admitted to college but could not enroll because of her inability to afford it: "I applied for scholarships and nothing was happening," she said. "I was stressed . . . losing weight." After waiting a year, Lydia was able to secure support to attend school from members of her community, but Lydia's predicament illustrates how even resilience may not be enough without the help of others. Lydia's story makes clear that while the ability to overcome odds should be celebrated, it is important to recognize that these successes are not without clear costs. The fact that such costs are common for girls like Lydia should not lull us into thinking that such costs are acceptable. In other words, girls like Lydia should not need to be resilient. We simply need to do better.

Becoming College Girls and Graduates in Modern Ghana

What does college look like for girls who are the first to attend college in their families and do not benefit from attending a highly ranked secondary school? By the time these girl students are admitted to college, they have competed with students who are far more prepared, and, indeed, they typically struggle. Year after year, I would check in and see some of the top students from APSS, such as Ama and Lydia, receive the lowest grades in college, especially as they took more specialized courses related to their majors. While these students had a desire to do well and appeared to maintain a belief that they could, this desire and belief did not translate to high grades. In short, they had the right attitude but perhaps an inadequate aptitude.

These students left APSS with achievement-oriented identities which were critical for staying in school, but they no longer operated in an environment in which those skills were being developed and affirmed. Additionally, each year in college they struggled financially in an economic environment that was only getting worse. Finally, they had each come from a school that lacked the same level of resources and academic rigor as the schools of many of their peers.

Still, they persisted, and by May 2016, exactly seven years since the first day I met them, I received an invitation from Ama and Lydia to attend their college graduation ceremony in August. I was unable to attend, so I asked a colleague to go on my behalf. Happily, he agreed. On the day of the graduation, he travelled four hours to Cape Coast and made his way through the large crowd. Ama spotted him and waved him down. After taking several photos with her, he asked after Lydia. As neither Ama nor my colleague were able to find her at the ceremony, I sent Lydia an email to congratulate her. Weeks later, I finally heard back: "I missed the ceremony because I could not pay for the graduation fee on time."

My heart stopped. After enduring so much to be the first in her family to attend and graduate college, a fee, the equivalent of 75 US dollars, kept her from attending her own graduation.

Did Lydia lack grit? Did her grittiness run out? Not at all. Like many poor girls, her objective conditions continued, and will continue, to constrain her life chances. It is unfortunate that a single young person should be expected to have the fortitude to withstand it all.

In the end, Lydia did what she said she would do and graduated college, whether her struggle was fueled by self-belief or self-delusion or something else entirely. Still, her story acts as a reminder that, while these noncognitive skills matter, the development of these skills should occur in a society in which girls, regardless of their economic status, can thrive. Nonetheless, achievement-oriented identities, honed in schools, improve a school's ability to produce girl students who can be confident, strategic, and transgressive until the day they no longer have to be.

The Limits of Confidence
and the Problem with Achievement

Achievement brings its own anticlimax.

—MAYA ANGELOU

CONFIDENCE MATTERS. In the previous chapters, I discuss the importance of instilling confidence for building achievement-oriented identities. Examining South Africa, I document how the country's institution of a life-skills curriculum was used to instill self-confidence across primary schools, in part as a mechanism for reporting girls' experiences with violence. Turning to the United States, I show how Principal Knight positions success as "not about intellectual ability" but rather confidence. In the Ghana case study, I discuss how Headmistress Mary emphasized the ways in which confidence enabled her female students to "stand in front of the school and give a speech without winking," "rub shoulders with the guys," and get "excited whenever [she threw] a challenge to them."

And indeed, a general belief in the power of confidence and other noncognitive skills is nothing new. It has spurred a plethora of research initiatives on the topic from scholars and practitioners alike. Most of these initiatives suggest that confidence, in addition to factors such as discipline, grit, and self-control, closes gender gaps in education and career achievement.[1]

Nonetheless, in contrast to the standard belief in the power of confidence, I explain in this chapter why an overemphasis on confidence—and likely on any other individual trait—is not enough to explain the academic and net achievement of girls. In short, confidence matters, but not that much.

To make this case, I engage in an analysis of data commonly used to measure academic achievement, specifically. I show how performance gaps between girls and boys remain, regardless of confidence levels. In documenting this finding, I illustrate that these performance gap measures do not explain much because they ignore social conditions. I conclude, therefore, that academic evaluations which rely on factors such as confidence are insufficient for addressing academic inequities. But before I get ahead of myself, let us briefly review the literature on the value of confidence.

The Role of Confidence
for Academic Achievement

Let's start with assessments in the United States. Over twenty years ago, the American Association of University Women (AAUW) released a report that brought national attention to the disparity in confidence between boys and girls in the United States. The first of its kind, the study surveyed nearly 3,000 boys and girls (2,374 girls and 600 boys) between ages nine and fifteen and between grades four and ten from different racial and ethnic backgrounds. The children were asked ninety-two questions related to self-perception, educational experiences, interest in math and science, and aspirations. The findings revealed that, while boys and girls both experience a decline in their confidence and self-esteem as they get older, girls experience not only a more significant drop but a more lasting one. The significant and lasting drop in girls' confidence and self-esteem likely shaped their unequal academic achievement.[2]

More specifically, the study revealed that many girls express a high level of self-esteem around ages eight and nine. However, by the time they leave high school their reported self-esteem declines more than 30 percent (from 60 percent to 29 percent), whereas boys experience a decline of 21 percent (from 69 percent to 46 percent). Accordingly, nearly half of boys enter adulthood reporting high self-esteem while more than 70 percent of girls do not.[3]

The report based on the survey suggested that this lack of self-esteem may affect the academic subjects girls express interest in, how they act in the classroom, and what they think of themselves in the future. This is supported by results showing that boys are more likely to speak up in class or correct the teacher if they believe he or she is wrong. In addition, survey results revealed that girls are less likely to report that they are happy the way they are or that they are good at a lot of things.[4]

The survey focused on the areas of math and science. These are the subjects in which girls experience the highest level of academic and career disparities. In addition, the number of available occupations in these fields was expected to soar. Regarding these subjects, the survey revealed that "as girls learn that they are not good at these subjects [math and science], their sense of self-worth and aspirations for themselves deteriorate."[5] More specifically, while boys may view the subject of math as too hard and not useful, girls see their difficulties with math as a personal failing.[6]

One of the most interesting aspects of the AAUW survey is its finding that family and school experiences are the main factors in shaping self-esteem and confidence. In particular, they find that a girl's self-esteem improves when she believes that her family or her teachers believe she can do something. To further investigate this claim, Peggy Orenstein examined the specific educational experiences of schoolgirls as they transitioned into adolescence in her book *Schoolgirls: Young Women, Self-Esteem, and the Confidence Gap.* Using the AAUW survey as a basis, Orenstein engaged in an in-depth qualitative investigation of schoolgirls from different racial and ethnic backgrounds across two West Coast middle schools. She documents how schools actively aid in the development of a hidden curriculum that teaches girls to be passive and boys to be assertive.[7] Girls internalize these negative ideas, which in turn take a toll on their self-image, self-confidence, and ultimately their ability to lead full and satisfying lives.

Yet the AAUW study found some compelling differences across race that remain unresolved, even after Orenstein's study. The AAUW findings revealed that Black girls were more likely than White or Latina girls to retain their confidence through high school and report being happy with the way they were. In fact, Latina girls experienced the steepest decline in self-esteem between the ages of nine and fifteen (a decline of 38 percent, from 68 percent to 30 percent) compared with White girls (a decline of 33 percent, from 55 percent to 22 percent) and Black girls (a decline of 7 percent, from 65 percent to 58 percent).[8] Although no surveys of the same scope and scale have been conducted since the 1992 AAUW report, research consistently shows that Black girls tend to express higher confidence than their White and Latina peers as they get older.[9]

Black girls may display a higher level of confidence in their abilities and aspirations regarding math and science, but compared with White and Hispanic girls, their performance in these subjects does not mirror those of their majority counterparts.[10] If confidence is the key and if Black girls have it, then why aren't they doing just as well or better than their White and Latina peers? Suggestively, the AAUW study found that Black girls in the United States were more likely than their peers to report negative attitudes toward their teachers and school. Confidence, then, did not preclude negative perceptions of their educational experience.[11]

Studies in west and southern Africa suggest that girls' experiences in the classroom inhibit their confidence and subsequent academic achievement gradually. In Ghana, for example, country-level analysis shows a gradual decline in mathematics performance of girls that accelerates as they enter high school.[12] There is evidence that confidence plays a role in this disparity. In junior high, girls and boys express equally positive attitudes toward math. This changes for girls once they enter high school.[13] In high school girls begin to take more stereotypically gendered classes, such as home economics, while boys are steered toward math and science. Just like girls in the United States, the decision by girls to enroll in home science courses versus math courses is influenced by their school and class environment, in addition to their relationship with adults in their families and at school.[14] Accordingly, girls may adhere to advice provided by these individuals—regardless of gender identification—that pushes them to take on certain subjects while completely avoiding others. Boys, on the other hand, are encouraged not to take on fields viewed as exclusive to girls, such as home economics. Furthermore, boys have more space to contest decisions with which they do not agree.[15] Findings across the United States and Africa provide compelling evidence that the school and community's ability to increase the confidence of its girls by encouraging them to take on educational challenges can play an important role in, at the very least, narrowing academic disparities between genders.

The Continued Relevance of Confidence

It is unsurprising, then, that more than twenty years since the release of the AAUW report and Orenstein's book the discussion about the importance of confidence in helping girls achieve is still relevant. The focus on the confidence gap in the United States, specifically, regained attention in articles and books such as the one published in 2014 by Claire Shipman and Katy Kay.[16] Their work, like many others, revealed the persistence of inequalities related to career aspirations and achievement based on gender.

Some of the significant research they highlight includes the fact that women turn down twice as many opportunities as men and that they are equally, if not more, qualified for many positions. Lower confidence is singled out as the factor causing women to underestimate their abilities and performance relative to men. Thus, men apply for a promotion when they feel they have half of the necessary qualifications, but women wait until their qualifications are essentially undeniable.[17] This research acknowledges that women are often aware of the negative reactions that sometimes come from society when they do stand up, speak out, and project confidence in the same way that men do. Nonetheless, Kay and Shipman conclude that the confidence gap explains existing disparities between men and women well into their careers. Confidence, they claim, shapes success almost as much as competence.[18] If we accept this theory, then, increasing the confidence of women and girls should contribute to more equitable academic and career outcomes not only in the United States but also in many other countries where women and girls experience barriers to success (even if it does not explain the specific case of Black girls).

The Problem with Confidence

For years researchers have been concerned with cataloging and quantifying what qualities guarantee success in an individual, particularly in girls, around the globe. Confidence has been tagged as a likely fundamental mechanism to close academic achievement and career gaps. Singling out confidence, however, requires that we adopt two problematic assumptions. First, we would need to believe that achievement should be measured merely by individual performance and not by processes or experiences. Second, we would have to accept that success could be predicated on a single factor rather than a system or set of systems. When we adopt these problematic assumptions, we place the source of achievement inequities on a defect in the individual (for example, low confidence) and thus contribute to the development of thin solutions based on removing the defect (for example, increasing her confidence) rather than improving the context by dismantling the patriarchal structure in which girls and women find themselves.

Furthermore, while academic achievement is important, it is an insufficient measure of success in that it ignores costs borne. In other words, traditional evaluations of achievement can be useful but are not wholly descriptive, given their lack of engagement with students' social, emotional, and physical experiences. An increasing number of studies highlight how students who come from disadvantaged backgrounds neglect their physical and emotional well-being as they work toward defying the odds stacked against them to become high academic achievers. In addition, they face additional barriers based on their race, gender, and economic status as they rise through the ranks, which requires them to double their efforts. The result is that these students become relatively more successful than their fellow disadvantaged peers but also less healthy. In short, they pay for their success by sacrificing their health.[19]

A more productive focus for schools would be the measurement of students' net achievement—a type of achievement that accounts for the social, emotional, and physical costs of student's educational experience and context. A measure of net achievement acknowledges the limits of traditional measures of academic performance. It concedes that proposed individual-level factors, such as confidence, are used as holy-grail solutions to resolving educational disparities. It asks the same question posed in Chapter 1 regarding the experiences of Zeneba and Kai: If a low-income student earns high grades but experiences trauma in the process, has that student achieved?

To demonstrate the limits of confidence and measures of academic achievement, I analyze data from the 2011 Trends in International Mathematics and Science Study (TIMSS). I use these data across South Africa, the United States, and Ghana to evaluate gender differences in math and, to a lesser extent, science performance.[20] While making direct comparisons is difficult given the many variations across these different countries, I examine the same or similar factors in each country-level analysis.[21] In doing so, I demonstrate how confidence barely explains academic achievement across different contexts, gender groups, and racial groups. I offer an explanation as to why these exercises are futile before putting forth the concept of net achievement for future analysis.

Data and Analysis

Created in 1995, TIMSS is an international comparative assessment of academic achievement in math and science of more than sixty countries. Assessments are conducted every four years and include contextual factors such as students' home resources as well as interest and confidence in these subjects. Countries choose to participate in each cycle. The data are collected by Boston College's Lynch School of Education in collaboration with in-country officers. The results are categorized into four benchmarks: Advanced (625), High (550), Intermediate (475), and Low (400).[22] The mean score is a 500, with a 100-point standard deviation.

For the analysis, I compare students between fourth and eighth grade who range in confidence levels from low to high toward math and science and try to determine how their confidence levels affect their academic achievement in these subjects. In making these comparisons, I do my best to account for other factors that I expect to matter, including race, gender, and socioeconomic context (at school and at home).[23] By doing so, I attempt to determine how confidence may or may not narrow gaps for Black middle-class girls versus poor Latina girls, for example, instead of assuming that "girls" as a category account for all girls' backgrounds and experiences.

I present the findings by providing for each country a brief description of its education sector followed by its specific participation in the TIMSS data analysis. I then report the findings first by gender, confidence, and achievement, adding both individual- and contextual (school)-level measures of economic status and education. Thereafter, if applicable and where data are available, I provide the same analysis broken down by race.

It is important to note that TIMSS has been critiqued for its standardized nature, as African countries have to adjust to a style of testing they did not have a hand in developing. TIMSS data, therefore, may not accurately reflect academic achievement in math and science. For my purposes, the value of each country's test scores, and whether they score high or low compared with other countries, is not central to the analysis. Instead, I use the data as a mechanism to better understand the ways in which confidence and socioeconomic background work together to shape differences in achievement between boys and girls within a country (regardless of what that actual achievement is). My hope is that we may develop an understanding of similarities across these various contexts and perceive the limits of these types of analyses.

SOUTH AFRICA

Since collection of TIMSS data began in 1994, South Africa has continued to be among the worst-performing countries, alongside Saudi Arabia, Morocco, Jordan, and Kuwait. As recently as 2015, between 50 percent and 60 percent of learners in South Africa scored below a 400—100 points below the average score. Still, these numbers represent a significant increase in academic performance over the past few years—up nearly ninety points from 2011.[24] Furthermore, these increases were made mostly at the lower end of the distribution, with public school (fee and no-fee) students achieving the greatest gains.

The recent increases in performance among those within the lower end of the distribution is may be attributed in part to the proportion of the population with a higher education degree, which has increased from 24 percent to 41 percent. Students also report higher levels of teacher satisfaction and student belonging. An increase in school attendance also made a positive impact in academic scores. Being absent from school once a week or more was associated with a sixty-four-point decrease in math and an eighty-four-point decrease in science. In addition, those who attended schools that emphasized academic success scored thirty-four points higher in math and thirty-eight points higher in science. Still, most relevant for this chapter, increases in scores were coupled by increases in confidence in science and math across South Africa between 2011 and 2015. More specifically, those who were confident in math scored eighty-nine points higher, and those confident in science scored sixty-five points higher. Altogether, confidence was associated with improved math outcomes, as was school attendance and an emphasis by the school on academic success.

Although I could not access data by race, race is commonly aligned with school type in South Africa. Blacks are more likely to attend non-fee public schools. Public schools represent 91 percent of the school system in South Africa, and independent schools represent 9 percent. In 2015, 70 percent of students in South Africa attended non-fee public schools compared with

27 percent and 4 percent who attended fee-paying public schools and independent schools, respectively. Of the 70 percent who attend non-fee public schools, 86 percent are recipients of government aid, 59 percent lack access to flush toilets, and 41 percent lack access to running water. The parents of those who attend non-fee public schools are 50 percent more likely to have no more than a high school education, and the effect of low parental education is evident in these students' academic achievement outcomes. On average, students from non-fee public schools score 344 compared with 445 for students from fee-paying public schools and 506 for students from independent schools. Confidence does not change this very much.

In terms of gender, the data show that girls outperform boys in fourth and fifth grades by sixteen points overall. By eighth and ninth grades, the gender gap between boys and girls essentially disappears. The apparent head start and subsequent decline of girls' academic achievement in the early years raise questions about what happens in the classroom at different stages of schooling. Girls are on track to do better as early as fifth grade, scoring on average fifteen points higher than boys, which is a statistically significant difference. By the time girls reach eighth and ninth grades, however, the gap narrows to seven points, a negligible difference.

In a robust study I conducted in collaboration with members of the Human Sciences Research Council in South Africa, 2011 TIMSS data were used to identify those students from poor families who attend schools with limited resources but are academically successful (defined as *resilient* students in Figure 4.1). Analysis of the TIMSS data showed that in South Africa girls are more likely to achieve academically despite their poor background if they expressed confidence in their ability to learn mathematics *and* if they exhibited positive attitudes toward their learning environment.[25] Nonetheless, the analysis revealed that girl students in South Africa must be resilient to achieve (for ex-

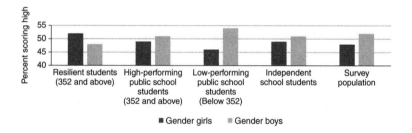

FIGURE 4.1. Performance in math by gender and school type—South Africa
Data source: 2011 TIMSS.

Note: Using simple cross tabulation analysis or each group, we estimated the percentage of learners with these specific characteristics. This was followed by a chi-square test that indicated statistical significance ($p < .05$) for all the variables. See G. Frempong, M. Visser, N. Feza, L. Winnaar, and S. Nuamah, "Resilient Learners in Schools Serving Poor Communities." *Electronic Journal of Research in Educational Psychology* 14, no. 39: 352–367.

ample, withstanding bullying and sexual assault). Even if a girl has confidence which contributes to her success, schools must create environments that are substantively gender equal to ensure that girls have positive attitudes toward their learning environment. Girls should not have to work harder to achieve the same results as their male counterparts or be stronger than boys to achieve; schools must to do a better job at crafting more positive educational experiences for all their students.

UNITED STATES

The United States has participated in TIMSS since 1994 and has continued to rank among the top twenty-five countries, scoring slightly above the international average of 500 among both fourth graders and eighth graders. The United States typically ranks behind countries only in Asia and Europe. In 2003, the TIMSS data revealed that US boys were still outperforming girls in math and science, although by a small margin. Furthermore, an analysis of 1999 TIMSS data, connected with the Programme for International Student Assessment (PISA), found that such differences were not significantly connected to self-perceptions of confidence, although girls were more likely to report lower levels of confidence in these subjects.[26]

By 2011, in the United States, disparities in achievement between boys and girls were essentially eliminated in math and for most science topics. Research published only a few years earlier suggested that these disparities would end as women became increasingly more accepted into traditionally male fields.[27] Additional research suggests that at least a portion of gender parity in academics is a reflection of the state of gender equality of the nation.[28] If this is true, growing levels of gender equality across the United States would help to explain the academic improvement of girl students.

Yet while the gender gap in academics in the United States is decreasing, major disparities continue to persist at the intersections of race and gender. In the United States, historically through the present day, minority groups continue to be underserved as the nation struggles to treat them equally. Girl students of color in the United States must learn how to navigate a country that acts both as a beacon of equality to some groups in some respects and as a symbol of inequality to others.

Gender equality in academics across the nation has become more common, initial studies in the United States suggest, but it is unclear how that applies to doubly marginalized groups. In South Africa confidence plays a significant role in reducing academic disparities, although the effect of confidence is conditional on improvements in the structural environment. Does confidence play a similar role for reducing disparities between poor girls of color and their White majority counterparts in the United States? Is the impact of confidence conditional on other structural factors? If so, which ones?

When accounting for the economic status of students' home and school environments, while income matters, results show that in math, unconfident eighth-grade girl students who come from middle- or upper-class backgrounds still rank thirty to fifty points higher than confident girl students from low-income backgrounds. However, confidence was associated with an increase in scores of girls who come from low- and middle-income backgrounds by seventy-seven points and reduced the gap between the performance of girls from low- and middle-income neighborhoods by seventy-six points. Even so, the factor that appeared to matter most was the economic background of the school. Altogether, a highly confident girl who attends school with more advantaged students gains a whopping 120-point increase in math scores compared with an unconfident girl from a disadvantaged school. Excluding race, it seems confidence is necessary but insufficient to achieve improved academic outcomes in the United States.

Accounting for race among eighth graders, highly confident White girls score only eight points lower than their White male counterparts, and highly confident Black girls score only 1 point lower than their Black male counterparts (not a statistically significant difference) in math. Yet, when comparing the math achievement outcomes of highly confident Black girls with highly confident White girls and boys, there is a gap of seventy and seventy-eight points, respectively. White students—boys and girls— score significantly higher than Black students, regardless of confidence levels (Figure 4.2). Interestingly, a Black fourth-grade girl who is not confident in math and who attends a school where less than 10 percent of the school population is economically affluent obtains an average math score of 489 compared with 485 for a Black fourth-grade boy. If more than half of the school population is affluent, the average math score for a Black fourth-grade girl increases to 531 (compared with 520 for a Black boy).[29] In short, affluence of the students at a school correlates with

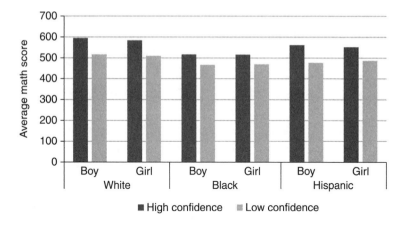

FIGURE 4.2. Eighth-grade math scores by confidence, gender, race—United States
Data source: 2011 TIMSS.

improving girls' academic achievement overall, but racial disparities between groups persist.

Yet, the gender disparity does come back into play. In fact, although being confident and attending a resource-rich school
contributes to overall improvements in the scores of boys and
girls, analysis of the TIMSS data suggests that economic advantage may exacerbate inequality in achievement by gender, regardless of confidence.

Indeed, across all racial groups, among economically disadvantaged groups, there were no statistically significant differences in
achievement scores in math by gender. However, as economic
backgrounds became more affluent, disparities arose across all
ethnic groups. In 2011, for example, for Whites, the average math
score for disadvantaged boys was 542 and for girls was 548, a
difference of six points. Among economically advantaged groups,
however, it was 572 for boys and 589 for girls, a difference of
seventeen points (Figure 4.3). For Hispanics, the difference in
average math scores was nearly twenty-four points between af-

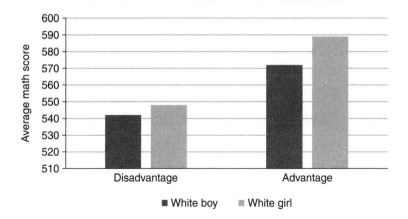

FIGURE 4.3. Eighth-grade math scores by economic advantage and gender on achievement for Whites—United States. *Data source: 2011 TIMSS.*

fluent boys and girls, compared with only four points between boys and girls who are disadvantaged.

Disparities also appear across race among Black and White girl students who share similar economically advantaged backgrounds. For example, affluent Black girls who are confident had an average score of 527 in math compared with 572 for affluent White girls who are confident—a nearly fifty-point difference. In sum, confidence and affluence contribute to improvement in math scores in the United States for Blacks, Whites, and Hispanics. These factors also significantly reduce gender disparities within race. However, confidence, and to a lesser extent affluence, do not significantly reduce disparities across race.

GHANA

Ghana began participating in the TIMSS data project at a sufficient level in 2003 using only eighth graders. At the time, the average Ghanaian student scored a 276, nearly 200 points below the international average of 466 (and higher than only one participating country—South Africa). By 2011, Ghana's mathematics score improved by more than 50 percent (as did South Africa's), due in part to an increase in time spent by students on homework rather than housework or employment, an increase in the education levels of parents, improved teacher quality, and the construction of more schools.[30]

While the improvement of Ghana's TIMSS scores indicates a positive shift in the academic achievement of Ghanaian students, disparities between boys and girls continue to persist at significant levels. For example, in an analysis of 2003 TIMSS data, George Frempong found that the students in Ghana who scored closer to the international average were almost exclusively boys from highly educated familial backgrounds. These same students were more likely to report that they like math, are confident in their ability to learn math, and view themselves as having high academic expectations.[31] Focusing on 2011 TIMSS data, we can see that many of these trends persist (Figure 4.4).

In 2011, of the eighth graders who come from poor backgrounds (most disadvantaged) in Ghana, high levels of confidence in math are positively correlated with higher scores in math when compared with those who express low levels of confidence; comparing girls only, there is an eleven-point difference and, comparing boys only, a thirteen-point difference. However, pitting genders against each other, boys who are poor but confident in their ability to do math score on average twenty-four points higher than poor girls who have confidence. Even boys who lack confidence in math score eleven points higher than disadvantaged girls who are confident and twenty-two points higher than those who lack confidence. In Ghana, confidence may narrow gender gaps in academic achievement, but boys ultimately have higher academic achievement scores. Confidence alone is insufficient.

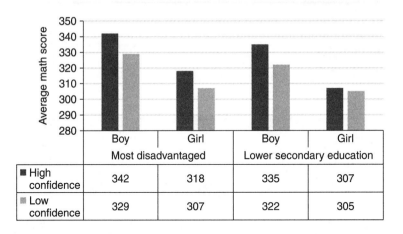

	Boy	Girl	Boy	Girl
	Most disadvantaged		Lower secondary education	
■ High confidence	342	318	335	307
▨ Low confidence	329	307	322	305

FIGURE 4.4. Eighth-grade math scores by confidence, economic status, education, and gender—Ghana. *Data source: 2011 TIMSS.*

With regard to economic affluence—a cumulative measure of parental assets—if a Ghanaian girl comes from an affluent background, her confidence in math is positively correlated with her mathematics achievement, while for boys, it does not make a difference. Accounting for affluence and education, the 2011 data show that a girl whose parents are college educated will do about as well in math as boys, as long as she is confident (Figure 4.5). However, the performance gap between boys and girls widens by thirty points if their parents only completed high school or no school at all. Boys may also score lower if their parents are less educated, but the difference occurs only between boys whose parents are university educated and those whose parents are not educated at all. Boys' confidence in math is associated with higher scores on the math exam across all conditions but girls attain higher scores on the math exam only if they come from a highly educated and, to a lesser extent, affluent family. In short,

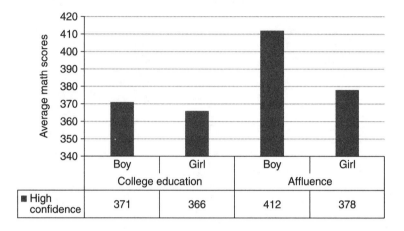

FIGURE 4.5. Eighth-grade math scores by confidence, college education, affluence, and gender—Ghana. *Data source: 2011 TIMSS.*

confidence does not improve the mathematics scores of girls with parents who are not highly educated and affluent. A close look at the data then suggests that girls in Ghana need a bit more than just confidence in order to do well in math.

The Advantages and Limits of Confidence

Overall, confidence plays an important role in improving academic achievement outcomes of students in South Africa, the United States, and Ghana, but it has its limits. In South Africa, boys and girls perform at a similar level in math and science (there is no statistically significant difference) in early school years, but girls are less likely to pass their college matriculation exams and, thus, enter college. South African girls are continually inhibited by concerns related to safety and the conditions of their non-fee-paying public schools, thereby forcing them to be resilient in more than just academics to succeed. Additionally, while data on race were not made available on South Africa, research suggests that serious barriers persist between South African girls who attend free public schools versus their White and Coloured peers who attend mostly independent (private) or fee-paying public schools.[32]

In the United States, confidence generally narrows the academic gaps between boys and girls. However, when race, gender, and economic status are examined, confidence plays a more conditional role for narrowing academic achievement gaps. For example, confidence closes the increasingly small gap for White boys and girls in math and science performance but does not close racial achievement gaps between Black and Latina girls and White students of any gender. Both Black boy and girl students who express high levels of confidence and aspirations in math and science still reach only low levels of academic achievement relative to their White peers. Economic affluence of a school or its students narrows the academic achievement gap across race but does not close it. In terms of gender, economic affluence contributes to the widening of the academic achievement gap within races.

In Ghana, boys continue to have an advantage over girls on math and science exams. Confidence narrows the gap but ultimately does not close it unless a confident girl also has a parent who is affluent and holds a college degree. When I compare eighth graders in Ghana and the United States in 2011, I find that kids who have parents with high-education backgrounds earn higher math and science scores in both countries and those who are more confident earn, on average, better scores. Yet, in Ghana, the score gap is forty-one points between students who have many resources at home and those who have few, while in the United States, the difference is nearly 100 points, suggesting wider economic disparities in the United States. This finding is consistent with more recent work by researchers at Stanford University:

"math gaps tend to favor males more in socioeconomically advantaged school districts."[33]

Across all countries, confidence matters. Still, as expected, it is conditional on various aspects of structural inequality, whether related to parental education, individual- or school-level economic status, and school experience. Most important, girls across these contexts are dealing with unequal gender relations that actively chip away at their academic achievement rather than build it. Given the various factors affecting girls' academic achievement, the analysis of the TIMSS data raises more questions than it answers. Clearly, a singular effort focused on building confidence to close the "achievement gap" by race and gender is not a viable solution. Improving individual academic achievement through confidence cannot save every girl student.

The Problem with Academic Achievement

Education evaluations such as TIMSS focus primarily on academic achievement, narrowly defined as a measure of cognitive skills and competencies. Little attention is paid to whether schools are fulfilling their social mission. Consequently, global conversations on education emphasize individual success over civic and social purpose.

Efforts to improve students' confidence are fed by a focus on individual academic achievement and high test scores. Seen through this lens, low test scores are tied to low individual achievement and do not take into account the wider impact of unfair power relations manifested in race, gender, and socioeconomic inequalities. This focus on individual achievement denies students an equitable education, for it ignores the larger systems of power that allow racism and sexism to flourish.

Focusing on a particular trait, such as confidence, as opposed to systems of power leads to the belief that some kids do not succeed because they do not deserve to succeed. Yet if a school cannot help an unconfident student succeed, this is a failure of both the school and society, not the student. The education system, in its ideal form, is supposed to control for the fact that kids come from different places but share an innate ability to succeed.

Controlling for the varied levels of preparedness among students does not mean developing programs to improve their individual characteristics. Recent research has made clear how programs that aim to improve individual characteristics, such as self-control, among low-income minority students have positive psychological, social, and academic impacts, but negative consequences on their health and well-being. These outcomes are in part related to their persistent encounters with inequality over time. In contrast, those who come from highly advantaged majority backgrounds do not experience these same negative outcomes.[34] It is unsurprising, then, that scholars who put the burden of proof on individual students' confidence and cognitive skills, rather than on society and its institutions, develop solutions that have little impact on those who need it the most.

Net Achievement as a Way Forward

There are alternatives to academic performance as a way of measuring progress. In addition to academic measures, solutions that center the practices of the institution ask students about the conditions of the school and whether it acts as a safe space for girls to learn; they ask about biases in school discipline procedures and gender-based hair and clothing policies; they ask about the availability of resources such as sanitary pads and toilets; they ask about gender-specific trauma services; and finally, they ask about students' perceptions of the overall well-being and the equity of their learning environment. The answers to these questions combine to form a measure of net achievement, of which individual academic achievement is but one part.

Ultimately, confidence matters, but it is an insufficient measure of equity unless tied to a definition of achievement rooted in the destruction of institutional racism and sexism. Accordingly, in addition to building confidence, schools must be invested in dismantling systemic racial and gender barriers that impact girls' educational experiences. They must teach girls how to strategically respond and transgress those same barriers they will inevitably encounter both outside of school and later, in the world. They must provide girls with the tools to form achievement-oriented identities and act as sites of social change that disrupt power and redistribute it. They must become feminist schools.

Conclusion

LETTING ALL STUDENTS LEARN

There is no such thing as a single-issue struggle
because we do not live single-issue lives.

—AUDRE LORDE

To let girls learn, schools must first protect them.
> That is, they must ensure that girls are safe from
> violence, trauma and fear.

*Then, they must teach them three skills: confidence,
strategy, and transgression.*
> That is, they must teach them to become achieve-
> ment oriented and thus develop a set of skills they
> can use to engage in a hostile world.

*Finally, they must reimagine what it means to
achieve.*
> That is, they must think about educational
> success as not limited to academic performance
> but rather as a holistic measure of costs and
> well-being, or rather net achievement.

*All three require schools to become equitable
institutions.*

That is, they must protect girls against undue
costs based on gender and provide them with the
skills to traverse the world thereafter.
Taken together, schools must be feminist.
That is: *how girls achieve.*

Until Then, We Persist?

Today, the prevalence of women's rights movements, including
#MeToo, #Time'sUP, #Bringbackourgirls, and #GirlRising, makes
clear the continued relevance of the challenges faced by women
and girls across multiple contexts—at work, at school, and at
home. More specifically, these initiatives reveal the specific obstacles women and girls face: general safety, sexual harassment,
lack of educational access, and barriers to achievement, even as
countries move toward gender equality. Still, these initiatives are
constrained by the dual messages they offer. Let's look at a recent example from the United States.

On February 8, 2017, during the US confirmation hearing for
Senator Jeff Sessions, a Republican from Alabama and soon to
be attorney general, US Senate Majority Leader Mitch Mc-
Connell invoked a rule that essentially allowed him to silence
Senator Elizabeth Warren, a Democrat from Massachusetts. When
asked about his action, McConnell said the following: "Senator
Warren was giving a lengthy speech. She had appeared to violate
the rule. She was warned. She was given an explanation. Nevertheless, she persisted."

The incident ended up backfiring on Senator McConnell. The
phrase *Nevertheless, she persisted* became a new battle cry for
women, many of whom could identify with the experience of
being silenced by men in public and private settings. When media

outlets praised Senator Warren for her persistence, the slogan took on a life of its own. Few at the time recognized that over-subscribing to such slogans can be as harmful to the mental and emotional health of women as movements built on phrases like "women can have it all" and "lean in." These slogans feed un-equal gender expectations, such as the belief that girls and women should be expected to simply persist in the face of gender biases because they always have.

It is also worth noting that daily predations and exclusions based on gender escape notice unless a key political figure or ce-lebrity is involved. The media—and with it, the wider world—pays attention to President Trump's "grab them by the pussy" comments, to multiple accusations of rape or abuse by Bill Cosby, Harvey Weinstein, and Justice Brett Kavanaugh, to Senator Mitch McConnell's silencing of Senator Elizabeth Warren. These atroc-ities happen *every day* to ordinary girls and women around the world—in classrooms, on subways, in cars, in bedrooms, and in bathrooms—without media attention or justice.

Indeed, as mentioned in Chapter 2, a 2018 US survey by Plan International revealed that 76 percent of girls aged fourteen to nineteen report feeling unsafe as a girl or woman and 69 percent says they feel judged as a sexual object.[1] A 2017 National Women's Law Center survey further reveals some of these everyday injus-tices that school-aged girls, especially girls of color, experience in the United States. The study revealed the following:

- One in seven girls reports feeling unsafe in or on their way to school.
- Over one third of Black and Latina girls surveyed have experienced someone in their immediate family being arrested or jailed. Only one tenth of a percent of Asian and White girls have had a similar experience.

- Nearly one quarter of Black, Latina, and Native American girls have been kissed or touched against their will.
- Nearly one third of Latina girls have missed fifteen days or more of school each year.
- Nearly half of Asian and Native American girls said someone used a racial slur against them (compared to 32 and 34 percent of Black and Latina girls).[2]

These findings highlight the multiple negative encounters that school-aged girls have with sexual harassment, poverty, and racism. Thus, while global messaging around "girl power" encourages girls to go to school, to report sexual abuse, and to become scientists, many schools remain unsafe spaces—sites of violence, trauma, and fear. In the face of this omnipresent suffering, we are offered narratives of resilience. Girls are told to have grit, "lean in," and persist. In effect, girls are left to confront the violence, trauma, and fear on their own.

With Rights Come Responsibilities?

Of course, the United States is not alone in its shortcomings related to the treatment of girls. I have detailed several other examples throughout this book, and I'll include an even more recent event from Ghana that is particularly relevant.

In March 2017, speaking at the 90th anniversary of "Speech and Prize Day," Ghana's Minister of Gender, Children and Social Protection, Otiko Djaba, gave a speech at Krobo Girls Senior High School:

> The teachers who impregnate girls, this is a serious warning to you. It is an abuse of their rights, and you are their role model. You must not be the one to abuse the

rights of the young girls. We must also put an end to child marriage. In conclusion, if you wear a short dress, it's fashionable, but know that it can attract somebody who would want to rape or defile you. You must be responsible for the choices you make.[3]

True, Minister Djaba acknowledged the very serious issue of teachers abusing young girls and expressed valid concerns related to teenage pregnancy, but her irresponsible conclusion exposed her as profoundly unaware of the ways in which sexism works. Data from the Gender Studies and Human Rights Documentation Centre (Gender Centre), for example, finds that one-fifth of girls in Ghana had their first experience with sex against their will, and nearly one-third have experienced sexual abuse over their lifetime (Gender Centre–Statistics on Sexual Violence in Ghana). The minister's advice to these girls is to wear longer skirts. And when critiqued for her comments, she defended them with an over-used trope: with rights come responsibilities.

This type of paternalistic rhetoric from one at the helm of gender advocacy emphasizes the need for a shared definition of what is meant by gender equality. Instead of properly attributing the source of the problem to society's unequal gender relations, Djaba put the responsibility on girls. Instead of considering what she, as the minister of Gender, Children and Special Protection, could do to stop girls' experiences with systemic, gender-based violence, she shames any girl who experiences violence by attributing it to the girl's choices. Instead of considering the fact that girls are disproportionately forced to confront burdens they had no hand in creating, she reinforces the idea that they are the ones who must change their behavior, not men.

This is not what feminism looks like.

In the United States and Ghana, well-intentioned efforts to improve the lives of young women and girls are circumvented by the inability of those in charge of these initiatives to take seriously the kinds of equitable institutions that women and girls need. Efforts have by and large focused on persisting through gender discrimination or to wearing longer skirts to avoid rape, placing the burden on the individual girl. As these examples and this book show, approaches that focus on fixing the girl rather than fixing her environment are harmful to girls.

Think Global

Too often, gender issues are described as global, but they are referring to the United States or to developing countries, but not both. To demonstrate why centering nonwestern countries in research on gender equity is important, I will use a recent and well-known example.

On January 21, 2017, women from around the world gathered to advocate for the protection of women's rights and thus human rights. Soon after, it was recorded as "the largest coordinated protest in U.S. history and one of the largest in world history."[4] Before the march, the committee members put forth a list of unity principles guiding the movement. The principles were organized under various themes: ending violence, seeking environmental justice, and securing reproductive rights, LGBTQQIA rights, workers' rights, civil rights, disability rights, and immigrant rights.

While these are principles that affect everyone, their justification for inclusion was supported by research on disparities in the United States. Women in America, for example, earn eighty-two cents for every dollar a man earns. Furthermore, nearly all the committee members were women from or based in the United States. Accordingly, although the women's movement had global effects, it was not by representation or by stance a global movement. This is important to acknowledge, though the goal is not to be divisive. The Women's March reflects the ways in which women's rights and feminist movements continue to be perceived as based in the West and then generalized to the rest of the world.[5]

When the United States implemented policies to improve gender equality through landmark policies such as the Nineteenth Amendment and Title IX, many developing countries did not realize these earlier successes, despite having "parallel feminist movements." In fact, it would be decades later before countries like Ghana and South Africa would adopt similar gender-based policies (for example, Millennium Development Goals in 2000 and Educate the Girl Child campaigns—United Nations International Children Emergency Fund, 2008). Nonetheless, this doesn't explain why the hegemony of US exceptionalism continues to trickle down into global social justice movements. Both the development of a Women's Manifesto in 1970 and the Women's March Unity Principles in 2017 were created without soliciting the advice of women in the Global South.[6] By continuing in this vein, the United States is inevitably privileging western issues, modes, and methods, instead of connecting and including women from around the world.

Accordingly, there is a need for western women's and feminist movements to acknowledge how their policies affect women across the globe and recognize the lessons they can learn from other countries. For example, few US activists may be aware that Rwanda's parliament is over 50 percent women, and South Africa's constitution enshrines gender justice as part of its constitutional rights. Finally, there is a need to establish connections among global women's struggles rather than treating them as separate and unfit for comparison.

In the end, women and girls face different levels of the same evil—patriarchy. It is incumbent on women everywhere to think about how recognizing our connections can help us move toward a more global and thus sustainable freedom for all.

Our Schools Are Unfit for Half the World

The global community continues to emphasize access and achievement for girl students, but it has ignored schools' inherited hostilities against girls' bodies and minds. To be sure, fewer schools explicitly restrict opportunities for girls. In fact, some of them even boast a higher enrollment and achievement rate for girls compared to boys and others. Still, nearly *all* schools carry forward oppressive legacies of sexism that distort girls' self-perceptions, violate girls' bodies, and place clear limits on girls' futures.[7] And so, even as girls gain access to schools on paper, they remain shut out of them.

If we think back to the story of Ezra and Jude, it is easy to recognize that many of us have met these girls before. Maybe we went to school with them. Maybe we taught them in a class. Maybe we passed them on the street. Maybe we are them.

Regardless of how or where, we've met them before. And we do them a gross injustice if we simply infer from their good grades and their stoic silence that they are doing just fine.

I can assure you that they are not.

What if I told you that they, like Jude, struggled to afford sanitary pads and thus missed school several times a month? What if I told you they were being sexually harassed in school or on their way to school every morning? What if I told you they were being overlooked and undermined in math and science class? What then would you demand that schools do?

Feminist schools ask two questions: First, how do our policies and practices levy disparate effects on a pupil's academic, civic, and social development? Next, how can we develop strategies to respond to these imbalances and thus ensure that students attaining the same education are not subjected to different costs based on gender, race, or sex?

To address these questions, feminist schools develop system-wide policies and procedures to hold themselves accountable to a simple formula: each citizen has equivalent inherent worth and should be treated as such. They re-orient the foundation of education in a way that prepares students to engage in a more equitable society while also preparing them to transgress and transform it because it is likely that an equitable society has not been achieved. They ensure that teacher and student interactions in schools not only build self-efficacy and strategic thinking through achievement-oriented identities but also enable girls to expect, promote, and create social change.[8]

Feminist schools, therefore, are important for providing the space and conditions for girls to feel safe and protected by disrupting power relations. But the feminist school is in service of the girl student's ability to have an equitable educational experience so that she can thrive in school and life. While the feminist school can control her educational experience, what happens when she leaves? The feminist school recognizes this dilemma and thus provides her with the tools—AOIs—that she can use to thrive in society as well.

This book conceives of schools as sites of social change and thus as institutions that can dismantle educational and societal inequities. By reforming dominant gender relations at the school level and imbuing students with the tools to be confident, strategic, and transgressive, feminist schools ensure that all students can attain net achievement and contribute to broader societal transformation.

Developing Achievement Networks to Support Feminist Schools

I am fully aware that schools are already overwhelmed with responsibilities and excessively blamed for a plethora of social ills they have no control over. In many contexts, schools, especially public ones, are contending with issues for which the state should have provided alternative social services, whether that be day care, health care, or other supports. Schools may be managing multiple responsibilities that should not primarily rest with them.

Even worse, across many contexts, public will and belief in the utility of schools continue to decline, contributing to further disinvestment in terms of resources and faith. Schools, then, are increasingly operating in a context where they are being asked to perform ambitious and noble functions without the financial support necessary to execute these tasks.

First and foremost, governments should prioritize schools by providing them with the resources and tools they need to thrive. Second, a school by itself is simply a building. It becomes an engine of education based on activities executed by those who work within and outside of it. To execute its activities, schools rely heavily on multiple stakeholders—volunteers, parents, community members, and local organizations. Thus, they are not simply the domain of the government, the teacher, the principal, or the student, but of the community as well. Bluntly put: you must get involved.

Involvement includes mentorship, volunteering, philanthropy, local school board participation, and organizing and attending community meetings. However, I also believe in a much more intimate involvement based on a fundamental belief that our fates are interconnected. We depend on each other, even if our starting points are different. Our investment in lifting up others is part of our civic obligation as citizens of the world. We must each absorb the potential individual costs associated with that investment for the sake of the collective good.

Many of those who are most disadvantaged wear that title largely because they lack the traditional supports, such as parental wealth and education, that correlate with individual achievement and success. By meeting our civic obligations, we can find alternative ways to provide these disadvantaged persons with similar support systems and with the tools they need to compete and flourish.

I call these alternative support systems *achievement networks* or *achievement net*s, defined as groups of teachers, peers, and community members who play a role in supporting disadvantaged students through their educational journeys. An achievement net is not to be confused with a safety net, however. A safety net is meant to catch people after they fall. Such services, such as foster care or child protective services, are extremely important and necessary, but they are reactive solutions. Achievement nets are proactive solutions that anticipate potential shortfalls by building an apparatus in advance. To be more specific, achievement nets are committed to supporting vulnerable students through the provision of social and material resources. In this way, even if girls lack *individual* resources at home, they can still get the support necessary to be academically successful through the *collective* resources of their broader school and neighborhood community. Achievement networks are made of individuals and organizations who see students struggling and take unconditional responsibility for them, providing them with the external support critical to academic and life success. With these tools students learn to draw the distinction between how they are being viewed in society and how they want to see themselves. Thereafter, education becomes the mechanism by which they can move from where they came from to where they want to be.[9] In other words, an achievement network acts as a necessary community-based supplement to the creation of feminist schools and thus achievement-oriented identities.

I offer a final story:

A few years after my initial research visit to Ghana in 2009, I returned to see how the girls I met were doing. It was then I discovered that Lydia, introduced in Chapter 3, had been admitted to one of Ghana's top institutions but would not be able to attend because she could not afford it. The total cost at the time was equivalent to 500 USD per year. Lydia applied for scholarships and waited, but heard nothing back. Finally, she decided to meet with the headmistress at her high school to tell her about the situation.

By the time Lydia left the meeting, Headmistress Mary had decided to take out of her personal savings the equivalent of three months of her salary to pay for Lydia to start her first year of college. She told me she just couldn't see Lydia's brilliance go to waste. Headmistress Mary acted as a member of Lydia's achievement network. Mary was far from rich and had no familial tie to Lydia. Yet, she decided to make sure that Lydia could be the first girl in her family to go to college. She believed it was the right thing to do.

Lydia went on to become the first girl in her family to graduate college. As I write this book, she has just completed a competitive summer leadership program run by the Harvard Business School. If Headmistress Mary had not acted as part of Lydia's achievement network, and if Lydia hadn't left school with an achievement-oriented identity firmly in place, her outcome would have likely been different. Fortunately for her, she will never know.

Shortly after learning that Lydia, despite being clearly qualified, had been almost unable to attend college, I started the TWII Foundation and began raising money to support Lydia and girls like her who were striving to be the first in their families to go to college. Since beginning in 2012, we have helped over thirty girls make their college dreams a reality. My goal is simple: I wish to be part of their achievement network.

Undoubtedly, many of us have benefited from people who acted as part of our achievement network—even if we did not call them that—of people, communities, institutions, and organizations who went out of their way to lift us up at critical junctures in our lives. When we serve others whom we barely know, unconditionally, we do our part to contribute to the long line of lifting. We do our part for those who need us the most. And by doing so, we ensure that disadvantaged students who were not supposed to be successful because of their address, their gender, or the circumstances of their birth can stand as examples of everyday young people working toward the better future that they deserve.

Change Worth Investing In

Lydia's story is a good one, but the goal is not for the Lydias across the globe to end up only at Harvard. The goal must be for girls everywhere to have the power to end up wherever it is that they want to be without bearing significantly different costs than their peers for doing so. As was true for Lydia, once provided with a safe space, any girl can achieve academically and personally, on her own terms, despite being born into this world at a disadvantage. With the tools offered by her feminist school, she can more strategically navigate the world and transgress the various spaces she enters.

To do this work, girls do not need to change or engage in additional labor. In fact, the opposite is true. *It is the work of the school to create the conditions for the girl to thrive.* Thriving involves having not only an equitable school to attend, but also the tools to navigate an inequitable society. In other words, given the unequal standing of women and girls in the world, the tools provided by feminist schools are to be used by girls to free themselves. And if these schools and the tools they produce are in fact equitable, they should be freeing for boys as well. Achievement networks support this goal.

A Final Word

In the end, whether it is developing gender-neutral hair and uniform policies, encouraging girls to transgress the boundaries of their femininity, or eliminating traditions that are, by default, only for males, feminist schools which develop achievement-oriented identities engage in the type of actions necessary to dismantle inequality and enable success.

These actions require feminist schools to take seriously the ways in which race, class, and gender constrain the achievement of all students, but especially some of its most marginalized populations: girls of color. By prioritizing its most marginalized populations, feminist schools engage in tactics that are based in fairness first and then expand outward. Thereafter, we must work as collective partners of an achievement network to provide feminist schools and their students with the specific resources they may need and support the specific tactics they may initiate, to be proactive in protecting girls from negative, gender-biased experiences.

When we don't protect girls from negative, gender-biased experiences, we deny those girls the ability to fully participate in a prosperous social, economic, and political life. Not only do we fail to acknowledge how policies affect boy, girl, and gender-fluid or nonbinary students differently, but we also fail to allow all students to be free in their femininity and masculinity, without fear. We fail to acknowledge society's role in keeping girls out of school through lack of resources, fear of teachers, and contrived suspensions over dress code or talking out. We compound the problem by demanding students solve such problems through "grit" or "resilience." We fail to acknowledge that the world is unfair, and thus allow the miasma of prejudice to dampen the potential of students to realize the full expression of their personhood.

A feminist school takes into account these threats to its pupils. It protects them, but it also teaches them to protect themselves and even to protect others. A feminist school inculcates self-belief and strategic action among its students, enabling them to transgress social norms and engage in social change. A feminist school allows its pupils, all of them, the safety to dream of a world in which they are no longer preyed upon for features over which they have no control. It provides its students with the skills to press this world closer to an ideal that uses each person's greatest potential.

In doing all this work, feminist schools ensure that all students learn. But unless they are built and supported, feminist schools are nothing but an idea.

The only remaining question, then, is not *why* we should build feminist schools, but *when*. The answer is, *now*.

Notes

Introduction

1. J. Dewey, *Moral Principles in Education* (1909; repr., Carbondale: Southern Illinois University Press, 1975), 7; italics added.
2. T. K. Tegegne and M. M. Sisay, "Menstrual Hygiene Management and School Absenteeism among Female Adolescent Students in Northeast Ethiopia," *BMC Public Health* 14 (2014): 1118.
3. United Nations Educational, Scientific, and Cultural Organization, Institute for Statistics, "Leaving No One Behind: How Far on the Way to Universal Primary and Secondary Education?" Policy Paper 27 / Fact Sheet 37 (July 2016), http://unesdoc.unesco.org/images/0024/002452 /245238E.pdf. The 130 million figure comes from https://www.worldbank .org/en/topic/girlseducation.
4. For more on these educate-a-girl campaigns, see Shenila Khoja-Moolji, *Forging the Ideal Educated Girl: The Production of Desirable Subjects in Muslim South Asia* (Berkeley: University of California Press, 2018).
5. J. J. Heckman and Y. Rubinstein, "The Importance of Noncognitive Skills: Lessons from the GED Testing Program," *American Economic Review* 91, no. 2 (2001): 145–149; A. L. Duckworth and D. S. Yeager, "Measurement Matters: Assessing Personal Qualities Other Than Cognitive Ability for Educational Purposes," *Educational Researcher* 44, no. 4 (2015): 237–251.
6. C. S. Dweck, *Mindset: The New Psychology of Success* (New York: Random House, 2008); L. Perez-Felkner, S. Nix, and K. Thomas,

"Gendered Pathways: How Mathematics Ability Beliefs Shape Secondary and Postsecondary Course and Degree Field Choices," *Frontiers in Psychology*, 8 (2017), art. 386; see also S. J. Correll, "Gender and the Career Choice Process: The Role of Biased Self-Assessments," *American Journal of Sociology* 106, no. 6 (2001): 1691–1730; N. M. Else-Quest, J. Hyde, and M. C. Linn, "Cross-National Patterns of Gender Differences in Mathematics: A Meta-Analysis," *Psychological Bulletin* 136, no. 1 (2010): 103–127; and L. Perez-Felkner, S. K. McDonald, and B. Schneider, "What Happens to High-Achieving Females after High School? Gender and Persistence on the Postsecondary STEM Pipeline," in *Gender Differences in Aspirations and Attainment: A Life Course Perspective,* ed. I. Schoon and J. S. Eccles, 285–320 (Cambridge: Cambridge University Press, 2014).

7. A. L. Duckworth and M. E. Seligman, "Self-Discipline Outdoes IQ in Predicting Academic Performance of Adolescents," *Psychological Science* 16, no. 12 (2005): 939–944.

8. On skills vs. dispositions, see V. L. Gadsden, "The Arts and Education: Knowledge Generation, Pedagogy, and the Discourse of Learning," *Review of Research in Education* 32, no. 1 (2008): 29–61, 43–44.

9. For more on well-being and learning, see M. Awartani and J. Looney, "Learning for Well-Being: An Agenda for Change," World Innovation Summit for Education, Qatar Foundation, n.d., https://www.wise-qatar.org/sites/default/files/asset/document/wise-research-5-eispptu-11_17.pdf.

10. J. U. Ogbu, "Understanding Cultural Diversity and Learning," *Educational Researcher* 21, no. 8 (1992): 5–14; H. Mehan, L. Hubbard, and I. Villanueva, "Forming Academic Identities: Accommodation without Assimilation among Involuntary Minorities," *Anthropology and Education Quarterly* 25, no. 2 (1994): 91–113; J. Boaler and J. G. Greeno, "Identity, Agency, and Knowing in Mathematics Worlds," in *Multiple Perspectives on Mathematics Teaching and Learning,* ed. J. Boaler, 171–200 (Westport, CT: Ablex, 2000).

11. Mehan, Hubbard, and Villanueva, "Forming Academic Identities"; M. A. Gibson, *Accommodation without Assimilation: Sikh Immigrants*

in an American High School (Ithaca, NY: Cornell University Press, 1988); N. Flores-González, *School Kids/Street Kids: Identity Development in Latino Students* (New York: Teachers College Press, 2002); N. Warikoo, "Gender and Ethnic Identity among Second-Generation Indo-Caribbeans," *Ethnic and Racial Studies* 28, no. 5 (2005): 803–831; N. Warikoo and P. Carter, "Cultural Explanations for Racial and Ethnic Stratification in Academic Achievement: A Call for a New and Improved Theory," *Review of Educational Research* 79, no. 1 (2009): 366–394.

12. Mehan, Hubbard, and Villanueva, "Forming Academic Identities," 97.

13. T. R. Buckley and R. T. Carter, "Black Adolescent Girls: Do Gender Role and Racial Identity Impact Their Self-Esteem?" *Sex Roles* 53, no. 9 (2005): 647–661.

14. The few exceptions are discussed in N. P. Stromquist, "The Gender Socialization Process in Schools: A Cross-National Comparison," paper commissioned for the Education for All Global Monitoring Report 2008, United Nations Educational, Scientific, and Cultural Organization, New York, 2007, http://unesdoc.unesco.org/images/0015/001555/155587e.pdf. Stromquist's comparative assessment of gender issues across schools around the globe concludes that "most of the attention to gender issues in education has highlighted the importance of *access* to schooling, while ignoring the considerable *socialization process* that takes place in educational settings" (p. 28). Stromquist states that "schools have yet to become major engines of gender transformation" (p. 6). C. Skelton, B. Francis, and L. Smulyan, eds., *The Sage Handbook of Gender and Education* (Thousand Oaks, CA: Sage, 2006).

15. C. B. Lloyd, B. S. Mensch, and W. H. Clark, "The Effects of Primary School Quality on School Dropout among Kenyan Girls and Boys," *Comparative Education Review* 44, no. 2 (2000): 113–147; Stromquist, "Gender Socialization Process."

16. C. P. Jones, "Levels of Racism: A Theoretic Framework and a Gardener's Tale," *American Journal of Public Health* 90, no. 8 (2000): 1212–1215.

17. See also I. Bohnet, *What Works* (Cambridge, MA: Belknap Press of Harvard University Press, 2016).

18. See L. S. Hansen, J. Walker, and B. Flom, *Growing Smart: What's Working for Girls in School* (Washington, DC: American Association of University Women, 1995); P. Mlama, M. Dioum, H. Makoye, L. Murage, M. Wagah, and R. Washika, "Gender Responsive Pedagogy: A Teacher's Handbook," Forum for African Women Educationalists (FAWE), Nairobi, Kenya, 2005, http://www.ungei.org/files/FAWE_GRP _ENGLISH_VERSION.pdf; L. Twist and M. Sainsbury, "Girl Friendly? Investigating the Gender Gap in National Reading Tests at Age 11," *Educational Research* 51, no. 2 (2009): 283–297.

Gender-responsive pedagogy in schools represents a notable African-based initiative that could be used in other contexts. While they promote schools that take actions to correct gender bias and discrimination to ensure gender equality and equity (Mlama et al., "Gender-Responsive Pedagogy," p. 2), they do not take the next step of giving girls the tools to fight inequities. They do not dismantle and redistribute power. Additionally, gender-responsive pedagogy is not tied to a reconceptualization of achievement where the values espoused in the theory would be taken seriously. Nonetheless, these kinds of schools are some of the best existing examples of educational institutions seeking gender equality.

19. P. Montgomery, C. R. Ryus, C. S. Dolan, S. Dopson, and L. M. Scott, "Sanitary Pad Interventions for Girls' Education in Ghana: A Pilot Study," *PloS One* 7, no. 10 (2012): e48274.

20. A. E. Lewis and J. B. Diamond, *Despite the Best Intentions: How Racial Inequality Thrives in Good Schools* (New York: Oxford University Press, 2015).

21. bell hooks, *Teaching to Transgress: Education as the Practice of Freedom* (New York: Routledge, 1994), 147.

22. C. Albertyn, "Substantive Equality and Transformation in South Africa," *South African Journal on Human Rights* 23, no. 2 (2007): 253–276.

23. S. A. Nuamah, G. Pienaar, and N. Bohler-Muller, "Gender, Socio-Economic Rights and the Courts: Towards Substantive Equality and Transformation," unpublished manuscript.

24. N. G. Alexander-Floyd and E. M. Simien, "Revisiting 'What's in a Name?': Exploring the Contours of Africana Womanist Thought," *Frontiers: A Journal of Women Studies* 27, no. 1 (2006): 67–89, quotation 74.

25. A comprehensive description and comparison of the types of feminism is a topic for another book. But here is some background: traditional feminism is often critiqued for its focus on middle-class White women, and thereby its inattentiveness to race, broadly, and its intentional exclusion of women of color, specifically. Accordingly, Black feminism became a mechanism to develop a theory that accounted for the experiences of Black women that were directly tied to racism and poverty. Black feminism seeks to resist essential notions of femininity and gender relations. As explained by the Combahee River Collective—an anti-racist, anti-sexist group of queer Black feminists—in their canonical collective statement of 1977: "Although we are feminists and Lesbians, we feel solidarity with progressive Black men and do not advocate the fractionalization that white women who are separatists demand . . . We struggle together with Black men against racism, while we also struggle with Black men about sexism" (Combahee River Collective, "The Combahee River Collective Statement," April 1977, reprinted in B. Smith, ed., *Home Girls: A Black Feminist Anthology,* 264–274 [New Brunswick, NJ: Rutgers University Press, 2000], quotation on 267). Altogether, Black feminism is meant to recognize that Black women's experiences with oppression sit at the intersection of race, class, and gender and act as an ideology / epistemology that advances women's rights through activism.

Alice Walker is credited with coining the term *womanist*—meant to be an umbrella term to describe an approach to feminism that also centers the experiences of Black women and women of color—in 1983. Deriving from Black rural older women referring to young girls who take on adult mannerisms as acting "womanish," like Black feminism it accounts for the experiences of Black women marginalized from the traditional feminist movement. While there is contention about whether one should identify as a Black feminist or Womanist, altogether *womanism* acts as a term that is inclusive due to its intersectional nature, its prioritization of the most marginalized, whether a Black feminist or a feminist of color, and its broader aspirations to be available to men and women.

Nonetheless, the term's origins, like those of Black feminism, are steeped in US-based scholarship, and thus it has been criticized as not fully representative of the experiences of Black women in the diaspora. Accordingly, Clenora Hudson-Weems coined the term *Africana womanism* to describe the unique experiences of women of African descent grounded in "African culture." She outlines eighteen items for the Africana womanist agenda: self-naming, self-definition, role flexibility, family-centeredness, struggling with males against oppression, adaptability, Black female sisterhood, wholeness, authenticity, strength, male compatibility, respect, recognition, respect for elders, ambition, mothering, nurturing, and spirituality. C. Hudson-Weems, *Africana Womanism: Reclaiming Ourselves,* 3rd rev. ed. (1993; Troy, MI: Bedford Publishers, 1995).

Three key differences between Africana womanism and other feminisms are: first, it is family and community centered rather than female and self centered; second, it recognizes the role of spirituality in the lives of women—where the natural and the spiritual are intertwined; and third, it views sexism as superseding racism, rather than as intersecting. Similar to womanism and Black feminism it celebrates elders, generally. In addition, it recognizes that since women have always worked outside the home, dismantling gender roles as described by White feminism is not applicable, nor does it take a separatist approach but rather views women's struggle as in alignment with men rather than in opposition.

As a Black-Ghanaian woman born and raised in Chicago—studying the experiences of Black women and girls across Ghana, South Africa, and North America—I take a Black feminist approach to understanding their constraints. That means I draw on the work of Black feminist writings that focus on the ways in which race, class, and gender interact rather than viewing them as separate. Indeed, Kimberlé Crenshaw's work emphasizes the multiple ways in which race and gender interact in the US context to marginalize the experiences of Black women, thus suggesting that it is impossible for a woman of color to separate one from the other. See K. Crenshaw, "Demarginalizing the Intersection of Race and Sex: A Black Feminist Critique of Antidiscrimination Doctrine, Feminist Theory and Antiracist Politics," *University of Chicago Legal Forum* 1989, no. 1 (1989): art. 8, 139. The ways in which these identities interlock as multiple components of subordination help to explain why Black women have a different material reality and consciousness concerning that material reality—they interpret it differently than others. See also P. H. Collins, *Black Feminist Thought: Knowledge, Consciousness, and the Politics of Empowerment* (New York: Routledge, 2002). Accordingly, when I say a school should be feminist, I am referring to the idea that schools should have values that address intersecting identities that both, separate and together, shape people's lives. In addition, these liberatory practices and ideologies should also resist heteronormative hegemony and oppressive economic systems, but that is a topic I examine elsewhere.

26. See also S. A. Nuamah, "Achievement Oriented: Developing Positive Academic Identities for Girl Students at an Urban School," *American Educational Research Journal,* in press; doi 0002831218782670.

27. M. Warrington, M. Younger, and J. Williams, "Student Attitudes, Image and the Gender Gap," *British Educational Research Journal* 26, no. 3 (2000): 393–407.

28. Consider this in light of the fact that many times we privilege those who adhere to hegemonic notions of gender and sexual identification and yet develop no programs or mechanisms for those who sit at the margins.

29. "South Africa Has One of the World's Worst Education Systems," *Economist,* January 7, 2017.

30. Stats Ghana, "Education Statistics." Ghana Statistical Service, 2012, http://www.statsghana.gov.gh/docfiles/enrolment_in_primary_school _by_region_and_sex_2007-2010.pdf.

31. A few important notes about my approach to this research: I conduct most of this work using qualitative methods because they enable a

human-centered investigation of the persons most central to this book, girls. As stated by the notable feminist scholar Patricia Hill Collins, "For ordinary African-American women, those individuals who have lived through the experiences about which they claim to be experts are more believable and credible than those who have merely read or thought about such experience" (P. H. Collins, "The Social Construction of Black Feminist Thought," *Signs* 14, no. 4 (1989): s745–s773, quotation on s759). My hope is that by centering the experiences of those who have lived through the events I write about, I can give credence to the claims of the book in a way that is authentic.

In addition, I examine girls across multiple contexts and age levels. Although this poses some empirical challenges, my goal here is to show how students can have consequential experiences as early as kindergarten and thus demonstrate why interventions must begin early as well.

32. In terms of key concepts and language, I define gender as a socially constructed way of assigning different social practices to men versus women. I define gender identity as a person's independent decision to identify with one gender, both, or neither.

This book takes a female-centered approach to feminism. I focus on the female body as separate from one's identity as a woman. This matters because it accounts for the fact that if I were a boy—if I appeared to be a male or was in a male body—there are certain privileges I would receive or experiences I would be more likely to be protected against, such as rape and sexual harassment.

My female body's interaction with the environment requires a certain type of labor—meaning that there is work that that I have to do to limit the male gaze, threat of assault, or even death. For example, Black women are most likely to be killed by their male partners, 4.4 per 100,000 compared to 1 or 2 for other groups. See E. Petrosky, J. M. Blair, C. J. Betz, K. A. Fowler, S. P. Jack, and B. H. Lyons, "Racial and Ethnic Differences in Homicides of Adult Women and the Role of Intimate Partner Violence—United States, 2003–2014." *Morbidity and Mortality Weekly Report* 66 (2017): 741–746. It is my view that the traditional female body is subjected to certain types of physical violence when traditional male bodies are not.

And yet, I do not believe that feminism *has* to be female centered. There can be multiple feminisms that do similar work in liberating people to be themselves, and there should be. Accordingly, even in those cases where I am referring to the female body, I recognize how the traditional gender binaries associated with policies related to the availability of bathrooms and its impact on menstruation, for example, can serve to exclude those who may not have been born with traditional female body parts.

33. Getting along in any society entails engaging in its practices, no matter how unfair or counter to what you believe, because it is simply inefficient to do otherwise. And so, we all partake as a rational strategy to survive. Acknowledging that the cultures from which we come constantly constrain us, I make no promises to be perfect.

1. Becoming Safe

1. "Zeneba" and all names of people and some places hereafter are pseudonyms.

2. "Kai" uses the pronouns *they, them, their.*

3. S. Prinsloo, "Sexual Harassment and Violence in South African Schools," *South African Journal of Education* 26, no. 2 (2006), 305–318, quotation on 312.

4. A. S. Erulkar, L. I. Ettyang, C. Onoka, F. K. Nyagah, and A. Muyonga, "Behavior Change Evaluation of a Culturally Consistent Reproductive Health Program for Young Kenyans," *International Family Planning Perspectives* 30, no. 2 (2004): 58–67.

5. K. Hallman, K. Govender, E. Roca, R. Pattman, E. Mbatha, and D. Bhana, "Enhancing Financial Literacy, HIV/AIDS Skills, and Safe Social Spaces among Vulnerable South African Youth," Transitions to Adulthood Brief no. 4, Population Council, New York, September 2007, https://assets.publishing.service.gov.uk/media/57a08coced915d3 cfd00112c/brief4.pdf.

6. J. Parkes, J. Heslop, S. Oando, S. Sabaa, F. Januario, and A. Figue, "Conceptualising Gender and Violence in Research: Insights from Studies in Schools and Communities in Kenya, Ghana and Mozambique," *International Journal of Educational Development* 33, no. 6 (2013): 546–556.

7. W. Baldwin, "Creating 'Safe Spaces' for Adolescent Girls," Transitions to Adulthood, Brief no. 39, Population Council, New York, May 2011, http://www.popcouncil.org/uploads/pdfs/TABriefs/39_SafeSpaces.pdf.

8. E. B. Fiske and H. F. Ladd, *Elusive Equity: Education Reform in Post-Apartheid South Africa* (Washington, DC: Brookings Institution Press, 2004).

9. M. Nkomo, ed., *Pedagogy of Domination: Toward a Democratic Education in South Africa* (Trenton, NJ: Africa World Press, 1990).

10. N. Carrim, "Anti-racism and the 'New' South African Educational Order," *Cambridge Journal of Education* 28, no. 3 (1998): 301–320.

11. Across Africa, single-sex schools have been associated historically with elitist origins and British colonial models dating back to the nineteenth century. Accordingly, they have generally attracted those from wealthier families seeking to segregate themselves or uphold traditional notions of masculinity or femininity.

12. For example, Pretoria High School for Girls, a public fee school in Pretoria, South Africa, founded in 1902, did not permit Black girls to attend until 1994. Unfortunately, even as the population in elite schools has grown more diverse, racist practices continue to inhibit girls' achievement. In 2016, the school received global attention when its students protested the school's discouragement of natural hairstyles, such as afros.

13. K. Truscott, *Gender in Education* (Johannesburg, South Africa: University of the Witwatersrand/NECC, 1994).

14. A. Wolpe, O. Quinlan, and L. Martinez, *Gender Equity in Education: A Report by the Gender Equity Task Team* (Pretoria: South Africa Department of Education, 1997).

15. P. Christie, *The Right to Learn: The Struggle for Education in South Africa* (Braamfontein, South Africa: Ravan Press, 1985); Carrim, "Anti-racism and the 'New' South African Educational Order."

16. ONE, "Status of Women and Girls in South Africa 2015," ONE Campaign, Washington, DC, August 2015, https://s3.amazonaws.com/one.org/pdfs/Status-of-women-and-girls-in-South-Africa-2015.pdf.

17. World Economic Forum, *Global Competitiveness Report, 2016–2017* (Geneva: World Economic Forum, 2016), www3.weforum.org/docs/GCR2016-2017/05FullReport/TheGlobalCompetitivenessReport2016-2017_FINAL.pdf.

18. "South Africa Has One of the World's Worst Education Systems," *Economist,* January 7, 2017.

19. ONE, "Status of Women and Girls."

20. J. C. Streak, D. Yu, and S. Van der Berg, "Measuring Child Poverty in South Africa: Sensitivity to the Choice of Equivalence Scale and an Updated Profile," *Social Indicators Research* 94, no. 2 (2009): 183–201.

21. K. Crenshaw, "Mapping the Margins: Intersectionality, Identity Politics, and Violence against Women of Color," *Stanford Law Review* 43, no. 6 (1991): 1241–1299, quote 1244.

22. E. Unterhalter, "What Is Equity in Education? Reflections from the Capability Approach," *Studies in Philosophy and Education* 28, no. 5 (2009): 415–424.

23. F. Leach, M. Dunne, and F. Salvi, "School-Related Gender-Based Violence: A Global Review of Current Issues and Approaches in Policy, Programming and Implementation Responses to School-Related Gender-Based Violence (SRGBV) for the Education Sector," UNESCO HIV and Health Education Clearinghouse, New York, January 21, 2014, https://hivhealthclearinghouse.unesco.org/sites/default/files/resources/schoolrelatedgenderbasedviolenceunescoglobalreviewjan2014.pdf.

24. Human Rights Watch, "Scared at School: Sexual Violence against Girls at South African Schools," March 2001, https://www.hrw.org/legacy/reports/2001/safrica/index.htm#TopOfPagehwww.hrw.org/legacy/reports/2001/safrica/. See also C. Mitchell, "Mapping a Southern Africa Girlhood in the Age of AIDS," in *Gender Equity in South African Education 1994–2004: Conference Proceedings,* ed. L. Chisholm and J. September (Cape Town: HSRC Press, 2005).

25. The Education Foundation Trust, *Edusource Data News* 25 (March 1999): 15.

26. E. M. King and R. Winthrop, "Today's Challenges for Girls' Education," Global Economy and Development Working Paper 90, Brookings Institution, Washington, DC, June 2015, https://www.brookings.edu/wp-content/uploads/2016/07/Todays-Challenges-Girls-Educationv6.pdf.

27. M. Sommer and M. Sahin, "Overcoming the Taboo: Advancing the Global Agenda for Menstrual Hygiene Management for Schoolgirls," *American Journal of Public Health* 103, no. 9 (2013): 1556–1559.

28. V. Reddy, T. L. Zuze, M. Visser, et al., *Beyond Benchmarks: What Twenty Years of TIMSS Data Tell Us about South African Education* (Cape Town: HSRC Press, 2015).

29. J. Kirk and M. Sommer, "Menstruation and Body Awareness: Linking Girls' Health with Girls' Education," Special on Gender and Health, Royal Tropical Institute (KIT), Amsterdam, 2006, https://www.susana.org/_resources/documents/default/2-1200-kirk-2006-menstruation-kit-paper.pdf.

30. ONE, "Status of Women and Girls."

31. S. Mashaba, "8% of Schoolgirls Are HIV Positive," *Sowetan Live,* March 14, 2013, www.sowetanlive.co.za/news/2013/03/14/28-of-school girls-are-hiv-positive. In 2004, it was estimated that 12 percent of South African teachers were infected with HIV/AIDS, with that number nearly doubling among teachers aged 21 to 34 years [J. Louw, O. Shisana, K. Peltzer, and N. Zungu, "Examining the Impact of HIV and AIDS on South African Educators," *South African Journal of Education* 29, no. 2 (2009): 205–217]. It is estimated to have increased to 15.3 percent per research collected by the Human Sciences Research Council in 2015. The impact of HIV/AIDS on the educational system in South Africa falls into many categories: 1) the demand for education, in that HIV/AIDS status affects enrollment and prioritization of school in the lives of families dealing with HIV/AIDS; 2) the supply of education as teachers become infected, thus leading to teacher absenteeism; and 3) the quality and management of education, in that investment in infrastructure and education is redirected to health interests [C. Coombe,

"Keeping the Education System Healthy: Managing the Impact of HIV/AIDS on Education in South Africa," *Current Issues in Comparative Education* 3, no. 1 (2000): 14–27]. Treatment Action Campaign is known for a 2002 Constitutional Court ruling in which "the South African government was ordered to provide anti-retroviral drugs to prevent transmission of HIV from mothers to their babies during birth." To learn more about its work, visit www.tac.org.za/about_us.

32. A. Case and C. Ardington, "The Impact of Parental Death on School Outcomes: Longitudinal Evidence from South Africa," *Demography* 43, no. 3 (2006): 401–420.

33. Prinsloo, "Sexual Harassment and Violence."

34. For example, M. Jukes, S. Simmons, and D. Bundy, "Education and Vulnerability: The Role of Schools in Protecting Young Women and Girls from HIV in Southern Africa," *AIDS* 22 (December 2008): S41–S56.

35. J. W. De Neve, G. Fink, S. V. Subramanian, S. Moyo, and J. Bor, "Length of Secondary Schooling and Risk of HIV Infection in Botswana: Evidence from a Natural Experiment," *Lancet Global Health* 3, no. 8 (2015): e470–e477.

36. A. E. Pettifor, B. A. Levandowski, C. MacPhail, N. S. Padian, M. S. Cohen, and H. V. Rees, "Keep Them in School: The Importance of Education as a Protective Factor against HIV Infection among Young South African Women," *International Journal of Epidemiology* 37, no. 6 (2008): 1266–1273.

37. See G. Frempong, M. Visser, N. Feza, L. Winnaar, and S. Nuamah, "Resilient Learners in Schools Serving Poor Communities," *Electronic Journal of Research in Educational Psychology* 14, no. 2 (2016): 352–367. This study was based on observations and interviews conducted at a half-dozen schools across South Africa in 2014. Each of the teachers included in the study had teaching experience ranging from three to twenty-six years and across subfields and grade levels (kindergarten through twelfth grade). The schools examined were selected for their ability to create spaces that enable their students to achieve equally, which I determined based on traditional measures such as passage rates as well as observational and interview data collected on achievement

outcomes and attitudes. I ask about their challenges and successes to determine what works for transforming their most disadvantaged students, especially girls, into academically successful learners, thus creating the type of achievement-oriented identities poor students need to succeed.

38. V. Reddy, T. L. Zuze, M. Visser, et al., *Beyond Benchmarks*.

39. G. Ladson-Billings, "Toward a Theory of Culturally Relevant Pedagogy," *American Educational Research Journal*, 32, no. 3 (1995): 465–491. According to Ladson-Billings, culturally relevant pedagogy must meet three criteria: "an ability to develop students academically, a willingness to nurture and support cultural competence, and the development of a sociopolitical or critical consciousness," 474. See also G. Ladson-Billings, "But That's Just Good Teaching! The Case for Culturally Relevant Pedagogy," *Theory into Practice* 34, no. 3 (1995): 159–165.

The claims in this book are consistent with that of culturally relevant pedagogy in that I uphold the importance of academic performance and the development of a critical consciousness. Furthermore, I similarly encourage students not to work within the current structure but rather to transform it.

I encourage a holistic approach to achievement that accounts for the burdens students carry versus the benefits they receive, particularly for low-income Black girls not only in the United States but across the globe. It's not just about language or culture; it's about sex, gender, and personhood—traits that even a culturally relevant school could easily ignore (See also D. Paris and H. S. Alim, "What Are We Seeking to Sustain through Culturally Sustaining Pedagogy? A Loving Critique Forward," *Harvard Educational Review* 84, no. 1 (2014): 85–100.

40. D. J. Flannery, K. L. Wester, and M. I. Singer, "Impact of Exposure to Violence in School on Child and Adolescent Mental Health and Behavior," *Journal of Community Psychology* 32, no. 5 (2004): 559–573.

41. Trauma-informed schools recognize that traumatic stress from violence at home is often exacerbated by punitive school environments. See Flannery, Wester, and Singer, "Impact of Exposure to Violence in School on Child and Adolescent Mental Health and Behavior." Accordingly, proponents of trauma-informed schools call for an educational structure

that is responsive to these traumas at all levels. See S. F. Cole, A. Eisner, M. Gregory, and J. Ristuccia, *Helping Traumatized Children Learn,* vol. 2: *Creating and Advocating for Trauma-Sensitive Schools* (Boston: Massachusetts Advocates for Children, 2013), http://www.traumainformed careproject.org/resources/htcl-vol-2-creating-and-advocating-for-tss .pdf; Substance Abuse and Mental Health Services Administration, "SAMHSA's Concept of Trauma and Guidance for a Trauma-Informed Approach," HHS Publication No. 14-4884, SAMHSA, Rockville, MD, 2014, https://store.samhsa.gov/shin/content/SMA14-4884/SMA14 -4884.pdf; M. Walkley and T. L. Cox, "Building Trauma-Informed Schools and Communities," *Children & Schools* 35, no. 2 (2013): 123–126.

42. Robert Morrell, "Silence, Sexuality and HIV/AIDS in South African Schools," *Australian Educational Researcher* 30, no. 1 (2003): 41–62, quote p. 44.

43. bell hooks, *Ain't I a Woman: Black Women and Feminism* (Boston: South End Press, 1981), 1.

44. Multiple studies reveal differences in how girls experience trauma— "sexual abuse and assault, physical punishment, and psychological distress"—in interpersonal relationships, and differences in how they respond to trauma, including heightened stress, depression, and anxiety. J. Flocks, E. Calvin, S. Chriss, and M. Prado-Steiman, "The Case for Trauma-Informed, Gender-Specific Prevention/Early Intervention Programming in Reducing Female Juvenile Delinquency in Florida," *Northwestern Journal of Law & Social Policy* 12, no. 1 (2017): 9; J. Riebschleger, A. Day, and A. Damashek, "Foster Care Youth Share Stories of Trauma Before, During, and After Placement: Youth Voices for Building Trauma-Informed Systems of Care," *Journal of Aggression, Maltreatment & Trauma* 24, no. 4 (2015): 339–360. These reports, however, focus on juvenile justice centers or residential schools for court-involved youth. For an educational context, see M. McInerney and A. McKlindon, "Unlocking the Door to Learning: Trauma-Informed Classrooms and Transformational Schools," Georgetown: Education Law Center, n.d., https://www.elc-pa.org/wp-content/uploads/2015/06/Trauma-Informed -in-Schools-Classrooms-FINAL-December2014-2.pdf.

45. To combat negative experiences and traumas, recent reports propose that trauma-informed education be not only culturally relevant but also gender specific. For example, a 2017 report on the topic in the United States gave the following recommendations:
    - "Account for differences in types of trauma experienced by girls based on their intersectional identity
    - "Acknowledge the social and cultural contexts in which girls experience trauma
    - "Ensure that interventions are culturally competent and trauma-informed with attention to the unique needs of girls based on gender, race, ethnicity, and sexual identity"

    See R. Epstein and T. González, *Gender & Trauma: Somatic Interventions for Girls in Juvenile Justice: Implications for Policy and Practice* (Washington, DC: Georgetown Law Center on Poverty and Inequality, 2017), https://www.law.georgetown.edu/poverty-inequality-center/wp-content/uploads/sites/14/2017/08/gender-and-trauma-1.pdf

    Important resources in the United States include the Trauma-Informed Learning Network for Girls of Color in 2018 (http://www.acesconnection.com/g/aces-in-education/blog/trauma-informed-learning-network-for-girls-of-color-launches-in-late-spring) and the *Safe Place to Learn* resource package in 2017 (US Department of Education, Office of Safe and Healthy Students. *Safe Place to Learn: Implementation Guide,* Washington, DC, 2016, https://safesupportive learning.ed.gov/safe-place-to-learn-k12). These initiatives must be tied together by a single vision that represents not only a reaction and response to violence, but also an aspirational way forward. Feminist schools, I argue, represent that unifying vision.

2. Becoming Feminist

1. This name and all names of people and some places hereafter are pseudonyms.
2. In the 1980s, girls' schools were deemed to be a central solution for improving issues such as confidence and sexual violence affecting girls.

Many were founded in the United States and United Kingdom. Some studies suggest that same-sex schools provide a better academic environment, free of distractions, for both boys and girls than do co-educational schools, particularly in the realm of self-esteem and leadership. A. Datnow, L. Hubbard, and G. Q. Conchas, "How Context Mediates Policy: The Implementation of Single Gender Public Schooling in California," *Teachers College Record* 103, no. 2 (2001): 184–206. On the other hand, studies on single-sex Catholic schools suggest that girls' schools do not significantly contribute to the academic performance of girls nor do they reduce students' exposure to stereotypical behavior. P. C. LePore and J. R. Warren, "A Comparison of Single-Sex and Coeducational Catholic Secondary Schooling: Evidence from the National Educational Longitudinal Study of 1988," *American Educational Research Journal* 34, no. 3 (1997): 485–511.

In one study, teachers at girls' schools were perceived by the authors to be "talking down" to girls, thereby creating a less challenging educational experience. V. E. Lee and M. E. Lockheed, "Single-Sex Schooling and Its Effects on Nigerian Adolescents," in *Women and Education in Sub-Saharan Africa,* ed. M. Bloch, J. Bekou-Betts, and R. Tabuchnick, 201–226. Boulder: Lynne Rienner, 1998. Additional studies documented that, unless a school was intentional about deconstructing gender stereotypes or creating a nonsexist environment, many of these schools practiced similarly sexist actions as co-educational schools but with fewer resources and less academic rigor. A. Proweller, *Constructing Female Identities: Meaning Making in an Upper Middle-Class Youth Culture.* Albany: SUNY Press, 1998; Datnow et al., "How Context Mediates Policy." Single-sex schools thus seemed to further disadvantage girls rather than act as beacons of achievement.

By the 1990s, single-sex schools became less popular in the United States. Most that remained were Catholic schools, with their students representing only 1.5 percent of the total student population nationally. More recently, single-sex schools have been proposed and implemented as solutions for disadvantaged minorities. One successful example is the Young Women's Leadership Academy in Chicago. A study conducted by the University of California–Los Angeles in 2009 used an annual freshman survey that included responses from 6,552 female graduates of 225 private single-sex high schools and 14,684 graduates from 1,169 private co-educational high schools. Results showed that girls at single-sex schools were more confident in math, scored higher on their SATs, and had more confidence in their computer skills. The findings suggest that today's single-sex schools in the United States may contribute to better outcomes for girls. L. J. Sax, E. Arms, M. Woodruff, T. Riggers, and K. Eagan, *Women Graduates of Single-Sex and Coeducational High Schools: Differences in Their Characteristics and the Transition to College* (Los Angeles, CA: Sudikoff Family Institute for Education & New Media, UCLA Graduate School of Education & Information Studies, 2009).

3. *Brown v. Board of Education*, 347 US 483 (1954).

4. S. F. Reardon and A. Owens, "60 Years after Brown: Trends and Consequences of School Segregation," *Annual Review of Sociology* 40 (2014): 199–218.

5. L. Musu-Gillette, C. de Brey, J. McFarland, W. Hussar, W. Sonnenberg, and S. Wilkinson-Flicker, "Status and Trends in the Education of Racial and Ethnic Groups 2017," NCES 2017-007, National Center for Education Statistics, US Department of Education, Washington DC, 2017, Figure 6.1 and Figure 4.1, respectively, https://nces.ed.gov/programs/race indicators/indicator_rbb.asp.

6. A. Spatig-Amerikaner, "Unequal Education: Federal Loophole Enables Lower Spending on Students of Color," Center for American Progress, August 2012, Table 1, p. 4, https://cdn.americanprogress.org/wp-content /uploads/2012/08/UnequalEduation-1.pdf.

7. US Department of Education, "Working to Keep Schools and Communities Safe," 2015, https://www.ed.gov/school-safety-previous.

8. M. Sadker and D. Sadker, *Failing at Fairness: How Our Schools Cheat Girls* (New York: Touchstone, 1994); D. Tyack and E. Hansot, *Learning Together: A History of Coeducation in American Schools* (New Haven, CT: Yale University Press, 1990); J. C. Madigan, "The Education of

Women and Girls in the United States: A Historical Perspective," *Advances in Gender and Education* 1, no. 1 (2009): 11–13.

9. "Gender Equity in Education: A Data Snapshot," Office of Civil Rights, US Department of Education, June 2012, pp. 1, 4, https://www2.ed.gov /about/offices/list/ocr/docs/gender-equity-in-education.pdf. Young women are enrolled at slightly lower rates in science, technology and engineering majors (p. 3).

10. Initiatives focused on girls have reemerged in recent years, particularly with the 2014 expansion of Title IX and the 2009 establishment of the White House Council on Women and Girls, led by Valerie Jarrett. These national developments have been followed by a number of policy and research initiatives on the topic at the state and local level, including the African American Policy Forum's work on Black girls who are victims of gun violence, part of the #SayHerName campaign; and the creation of the women's research collective, the Collaborative to Advance Equity Through Research, administered by the Anna Julia Cooper Center at Wake Forest University. Important studies have been written on school discipline—for example, M. W. Morris, *Pushout: The Criminalization of Black Girls in Schools* (New York: New Press, 2016)— and on predatory colleges—such as T. M. Cottom, *Lower Ed: The Troubling Rise of For-Profit Colleges in the New Economy* (New York: New Press, 2017). In addition, the National Women's Law Center and the Georgetown University Law Center developed surveys and reports on school-aged girls (A. Onyeka-Crawford, K. Patrick, and N. Chaudhry, "Let Her Learn: Stopping School Pushout for Girls of Color," National Women's Law Center, 2017, https://nwlc.org/wp-content/uploads/2017 /04/final_nwlc_Gates_GirlsofColor.pdf), "adultification" of Black girls (R. Epstein, J. Blake, and T. González, "Girlhood Interrupted: The Erasure of Black Girls' Childhood," Center on Poverty and Inequality, Georgetown Law, Washington DC, 2017, https://www.law.georgetown .edu/poverty-inequality-center/wp-content/uploads/sites/14/2017/08 /girlhood-interrupted.pdf), the *Trauma Informed Learning Network for Girls of Color* in 2018, and the *Safe Place to Learn* resource package in

2017 (see Resources section at the end of this book). Each of these initiatives is especially important because of its focus on the negative educational experiences of girls, especially those of color.

11. L. Musu-Gillette, A. Zhang, K. Wang, J. Zhang, and B. A. Oudekerk, "Indicators of School Crime and Safety: 2016" (NCES 2017-064/NCJ 250650), National Center for Education Statistics, US Department of Education, and Bureau of Justice Statistics, Office of Justice Programs, US Department of Justice, Washington, DC, 2017, https://nces.ed.gov/pubs2017/2017064.pdf.

12. M. Sickmund and C. Puzzanchera, eds., "Juvenile Offenders and Victims: 2014 National Report," National Center for Juvenile Justice, Pittsburgh, December 2014, https://www.ojjdp.gov/ojstatbb/nr2014/downloads/NR2014.pdf; US Department of Justice, Bureau of Justice Statistics, National Crime Victimization Survey (NCVS). National Center for Education Statistics, p. 2, https://www.census.gov/content/dam/Census/newsroom/c-span/2015/20151204_cspan_crime_schools_slides.pdf.

13. Office of Juvenile Justice and Delinquency Prevention Statistical Briefing Book, Juvenile as Victims, School Crime Victimization, August 7, 2017, https://www.ojjdp.gov/ojstatbb/victims/qa02201.asp?qaDate=2015.

14. For the National Women's Law Center data, see N. Chaudry and J. Tucker, *Let Her Learn: Overview and Key Findings* (Washington, DC: National Womens Law Center, 2017), 3, https://nwlc-ciw49tixgw5lbab.stackpathdns.com/wp-content/uploads/2017/04/final_nwlc_Gates_OverviewKeyFindings.pdf; UNESCO data for special needs, lesbian, gay, bisexual, or transgender girls can be found at UNESCO, "School Violence and Bullying: Global Status Report," United Nations Educational, Scientific and Cultural Organization, Paris, 2017, 8–9, http://unesdoc.unesco.org/images/0024/002469/246970e.pdf; for Plan International data, see "The State of Gender Equality for US Adolescents," September 12, 2018, 58. https://www.planusa.org/docs/state-of-gender-equality-2018.pdf.

15. E. J. Meyer, *Gender, Bullying, and Harassment: Strategies to End Sexism and Homophobia in Schools* (New York: Teachers College Press, 2015), 71.

16. Meyer, *Gender, Bullying, and Harassment,* 71.

17. M. O'Shaughnessy, S. Russell, K. Heck, C. Calhoun, and C. Laub, "Safe Place to Learn: Consequences of Harassment Based on Actual or Perceived Sexual Orientation and Gender Non-Conformity and Steps for Making Schools Safer," California Safe Schools Coalition & 4-H Center for Youth Development, University of California, Davis, January 2004, http://www.casafeschools.org/SafePlacetoLearnLow.pdf.

18. N. P. Stromquist, "The Gender Socialization Process in Schools: A Cross-National Comparison." Background Paper Prepared for the *Education for All Global Monitoring Report 2008* (United Nations Educational, Scientific, and Cultural Organization, 2007), http://unesdoc.unesco.org/images/0015/001555/155587e.pdf.

19. C. Skelton, "Boys and Girls in the Elementary School," in *The Sage Handbook of Gender and Education,* ed. C. Skelton, B. Francis, and L. Smulyan, 139–151 (Thousand Oaks, CA: Sage, 2006).

20. Deborah Youdell, "Sex–Gender–Sexuality: How Sex, Gender and Sexuality Constellations Are Constituted in Secondary Schools," *Gender and Education* 17, no. 3 (2005): 249–270, 268.

21. E. J. Ozer and R. S. Weinstein, "Urban Adolescents' Exposure to Community Violence: The Role of Support, School Safety, and Social Constraints in a School-Based Sample of Boys and Girls," *Journal of Clinical Child and Adolescent Psychology* 33, no. 3 (2004): 463–476.

22. B. E. Hamilton and T. J. Mathews, "Continued Declines in Teen Births in the United States, 2015," NCHS Data Brief No. 259, Centers for Disease Control and Prevention, Hyattsville MD, September 2016, https://www.cdc.gov/nchs/data/databriefs/db259.pdf.

23. M. V. Harris-Perry, *Sister Citizen: Shame, Stereotypes, and Black Women in America* (New Haven, CT: Yale University Press, 2011); S. J. Ventura, S. C. Curtin, J. C. Abma, and S. K. Henshaw, "Estimated Pregnancy Rates and Rates of Pregnancy Outcomes for the United States, 1990–2008," *National Vital Statistics Reports* 60, no. 7 (2012): 1–21.

24. F. M. Biro, M. P. Galvez, L. C. Greenspan, et al., "Pubertal Assessment Method and Baseline Characteristics in a Mixed Longitudinal Study of Girls," *Pediatrics* 126, no. 3 (2010): e583–e590; A. Kale, J. Deardorff,

M. Lahiff, et al., "Breastfeeding versus Formula-Feeding and Girls' Pubertal Development," *Maternal and Child Health Journal* 19, no. 3 (2015): 519–527.

25. Morris, *Pushout*, 13.

26. J. A. Abrams, M. Maxwell, M. Pope, and F. Z. Belgrave, "Carrying the World with the Grace of a Lady and the Grit of a Warrior: Deepening Our Understanding of the 'Strong Black Woman' Schema," *Psychology of Women Quarterly* 38, no. 4 (2014): 503–518. Some studies suggest that multiple jeopardy builds their resilience (D. R. King, "Multiple Jeopardy, Multiple Consciousness: The Context of a Black Feminist Ideology," in *Words of Fire: An Anthology of African American Feminist Thought*, ed. B. Guy-Sheftall, 293–318 (New York: New Press, 1995); V. Evans-Winters, *Teaching Black Girls: Resiliency in Urban Classrooms* (New York: Peter Lang, 2005), thereby highlighting the agency Black girls are able to achieve even as they deal with systemic racism, classism, and sexism.

27. S. Fordham, "Those Loud Black Girls: (Black) Women, Silence, and Passing in the Academy," *Anthropology and Education Quarterly* 30, no. 3 (1993): 272–293; A. Henry, "Complacent and Womanish: Girls Negotiating Their Lives in an African Centered School in the U.S.," *Race, Ethnicity and Education* 1, no. 2 (1998): 151–170; M. W. Morris, "Race, Gender, and the School-to-Prison Pipeline: Expanding Our Discussion to Include Black Girls" African American Policy Forum, September 2012, http://schottfoundation.org/sites/default/files/resources/Morris-Race -Gender-and-the-School-to-Prison-Pipeline.pdf; Morris, *Pushout*.

28. Centers for Disease Control and Prevention, "Understanding School Violence: 2016 Fact Sheet," 2016, https://www.cdc.gov/violencepre vention/pdf/school_violence_fact_sheet-a.pdf.

29. S. Joe, R. S. Baser, H. W. Neighbors, C. H. Caldwell, and J. S. Jackson, "12-Month and Lifetime Prevalence of Suicide Attempts among Black Adolescents in the National Survey of American Life," *Journal of the American Academy of Child and Adolescent Psychiatry* 48, no. 3 (2009): 271–282.

30. M. Anderson and K. Cardoza, "Mental Health in Schools: A Hidden Crisis Affecting Millions of Students," NPR Ed, August 31, 2016, http://www.npr.org/sections/ed/2016/08/31/464727159/mental-health -in-schools-a-hidden-crisis-affecting-millions-of-students; A. Elster, J. Jarosik, J. VanGeest, and M. Fleming, "Racial and Ethnic Disparities in Health Care for Adolescents: A Systematic Review of the Literature," *Archives of Pediatrics and Adolescent Medicine* 157, no. 9 (2003): 867–874; S. H. Kataoka, L. Zhang, and K. B. Wells, "Unmet Need for Mental Health Care among US Children: Variation by Ethnicity and Insurance Status," *American Journal of Psychiatry* 159, no. 9 (2002): 1548–1555.

31. Epstein, Blake, and González, "Girlhood Interrupted."

32. Morris, *Pushout*.

33. D. J. Losen and R. J. Skiba, "Suspended Education: Urban Middle Schools in Crisis," Report, Southern Poverty Law Center, September 13, 2010, https://www.splcenter.org/sites/default/files/d6_legacy_files/down loads/publication/Suspended_Education.pdf.

34. "Data Snapshot: School Discipline," Civil Rights Data Collection, Issue Brief no. 1, Office of Civil Rights, US Department of Education, March 21, 2014, https://ocrdata.ed.gov/downloads/crdc-school-discipline -snapshot.pdf.

35. Musu-Gillette et al., "Status and Trends."

36. K. W. Crenshaw, with P. Ocen and J. Nanda, "Black Girls Matter: Pushed Out, Overpoliced, and Underprotected," African American Policy Forum and Columbia Law School Center for Intersectionality and Policy Studies, 2015, https://static1.squarespace.com/static/53f20d90e4b0b 80451158d8c/t/54d2d37ce4b024b41443b0ba/1423102844010/Black GirlsMatter_Report.pdf.

37. Epstein, Blake, and González, "Girlhood Interrupted," 7.

38. Epstein, Blake, and González, "Girlhood Interrupted," 8.

39. K. Kay and C. Shipman, "The Confidence Gap," *The Atlantic*, May 2014, 1–18.

40. *Womanism,* a term first used by Alice Walker in 1983, is a theory and movement that presents an alternative and expansion of the term *femi-*

nism with regard to Black women. It is meant to acknowledge sexism in male-centered racial justice movements and ideology, and racism in White middle-class feminist movements and ideology by centering the issues of race, gender, and class.

41. The school's version is adapted from *I'm Coming Out* by Bernard Edwards and Nile Rodgers, performed originally by Diana Ross.

42. S. L. Beilock, E. A. Gunderson, G. Ramirez, and S. C. Levine, "Female Teachers' Math Anxiety Affects Girls' Math Achievement," *Proceedings of the National Academy of Sciences USA* 107, no. 4 (2010): 1860–1863. It is important to note that close to 90 percent of teachers in the United States are female and have been shown to have high levels of math anxiety. R. Hembree, "The Nature, Effects, and Relief of Mathematics Anxiety," *Journal for Research in Mathematics Education* 21 (1990): 33–46.

43. This is not the actual name of the curriculum. The name is changed for privacy purposes.

44. While the various efforts at Teele Elementary have resulted in achievement-oriented identities and academic excellence for its students, I wonder if these same tactics would work for girl students in a co-ed environment. Indeed, the parents, teachers, and administrators I interviewed described the all-girls setting as beneficial for developing the type of environment critical for helping girls achieve. It is difficult to gauge what the results would be if a co-ed institution in the United States adopted these same practices. There is not a comparable institution that I know of. For more about same-sex schools in the United States, see note 2 in this chapter.

45. An important caveat: an all-girls school is not necessarily available to all girls. Teele Elementary, for example, is a relatively small school, which means that the demand for placement at this school far outpaces its capacity. Students are essentially selected on a lottery system unless they have a sibling who already attends the institution. Preference is provided to homeless students, students with special needs, and those who live in the neighborhood, thereby eliminating many of the weed-out tactics charters are criticized for. Furthermore, the school runs completely on the public dollar rather than outside philanthropy.

46. Morris, *Pushout.*

47. E. Baylor, "The Unlikely Area in Which For-Profit Colleges Are Doing Just Fine," Center for American Progress, November 29, 2016, https://www.americanprogress.org/issues/education-postsecondary/news/2016/12/01/291656/the-unlikely-area-in-which-for-profit-colleges-are-doing-just-fine/.

48. Cottom, *Lower Ed.*

49. US Bureau of Labor Statistics, "Labor Force Characteristics by Race and Ethnicity, 2015," BLS Reports no. 1062, September 2016, https://www.bls.gov/opub/reports/race-and-ethnicity/2015/pdf/home.pdf.

50. T. J. Matthews, D. M. Ely, and A. K. Driscoll, "State Variations in Infant Mortality by Race and Hispanic Origin of Mother, 2013–2015," NCHS Data Brief No. 295, Centers for Disease Control and Prevention, Hyattsville MD, January 2018, https://www.cdc.gov/nchs/data/databriefs/db295.pdf.

51. E. Petrosky, J. M. Blair, C. J. Betz, et al., "Racial and Ethnic Differences in Homicides of Adult Women and the Role of Intimate Partner Violence—United States, 2003–2014," *MMWR. Morbidity and Mortality Weekly Report* 66, no. 28 (July 21, 2017), 741–746, https://www.cdc.gov/mmwr/volumes/66/wr/mm6628a1.htm.

3. Becoming Achievement Oriented

1. This name and all names of people and places hereafter are pseudonyms.

2. While this chapter will use the case of Ghana to document several examples of girls like Ama persisting through challenges with the help of achievement-oriented identities, AOIs do not seek to perpetuate narratives of girls as resilient. Instead, AOIs seek to do the opposite by putting the onus not on a student's individual capacity to persist, but rather on the school's deliberate and intentional actions. In other words, a student's success or failure at a task reflects only the support provided by the school, not the student's inherent or independently learned abilities.

3. L. J. Griffin and K. L. Alexander, "Schooling and Socioeconomic Attainments: High School and College Influences," *American Journal of Sociology* 84, no. 2 (1978): 319–347; S. Raudenbush and A. S. Bryk, "A

Hierarchical Model for Studying School," *Sociology of Education* 59, no. 1 (1986): 1–17. I define noncognitive skills as including any trait, quality, characteristic, or factor which can contribute to academic achievement but that is traditionally left unmeasured on standardized exams. Scholars acknowledge the false dichotomy associated with pitting the two against one another: "Few aspects of human behavior are devoid of cognition." L. Borghans, A. L. Duckworth, J. J. Heckman, and B. Ter Weel, "The Economics and Psychology of Personality Traits," *Journal of Human Resources* 43, no. 4 (2008): 972–1059, 974.

4. G. J. S. Dei, "Education and Socialization in Ghana," *Creative Education* 2, no. 2 (2011): 96–105; C. Dweck, G. M. Walton, and G. L. Cohen, "Academic Tenacity: Mindsets and Skills That Promote Long-Term Learning," Report, Bill and Melinda Gates Foundation, Seattle, 2014, http://k12education.gatesfoundation.org/download/?Num =2807&filename=30-Academic-Tenacity.pdf.

5. G. Frempong, "Equity and Quality Mathematics Education within Schools: Findings from TIMSS Data for Ghana," *African Journal of Research in Mathematics, Science and Technology Education* 14, no. 3 (2010): 50–62.

In a study on same-sex schools in Ghana, researchers analyzed the relationship between confidence and anxiety on achievement for boys and girls in single-sex and co-educational schools. The study included 1,419 students across twelve secondary schools in the central and western region of Ghana. It revealed that girls in co-educational schools report high levels of anxiety and low levels of confidence in their ability to do math compared with girls in single-sex schools. Specifically, 51.7 percent of girls at co-educational schools expressed confident attitudes toward mathematics compared with 84 percent in single-sex schools—a difference of more than thirty percentage points. While boys in single-sex schools also expressed higher levels of confidence compared with boys at co-educational schools, the difference was smaller, at about ten percentage points. In short, single-sex schools in Ghana acted as important spaces for building girls' confidence in math. B. Eshun, "Sex-Differences in Attitude of Students towards Mathematics in Secondary

Schools," *Mathematics Connection* 4, no. 1 (2004): 1–13. Another study (V. E. Lee and M. E. Lockheed, "Single-Sex Schooling and Its Effects on Nigerian Adolescents," in *Women and Education in Sub-Saharan Africa,* ed. M. Bloch, J. Bekou-Betts, and R. Tabuchnick, 201–226. Boulder: Lynne Rienner, 1998) found that girls in Nigeria perform better in math in single-sex schools than in co-educational schools. They also participate more in class and are more likely to take on careers in math and science. S. Y. Erinosho, "The Making of Nigerian Women Scientists and Technologists." *Journal of Career Development* 24, no. 1 (1997): 71–80. Nonetheless, it is unclear that there *must* be a single-sex setting for these positive outcomes to occur. It is more likely the case that the practices of the school, whether single sex or co-educational, must enable these positive behaviors.

6. M. Frye, "Bright Futures in Malawi's New Dawn: Educational Aspirations as Assertions of Identity," *American Journal of Sociology* 117, no. 6 (2012): 1565–1624.

7. K. Akyeampong, "Public-Private Partnership in the Provision of Basic Education in Ghana: Challenges and Choices," *Compare* 39, no. 2 (2009): 135–149.

8. This number changes significantly once we account for the rural areas and the northern region of the country, albeit to a much smaller degree at the primary level than at any other level of education. For more information, see Ghana Statistical Service's (2006) Education Statistics website at www.statsghana.gov.gh/edu_stats.html.

9. A 2017 policy from the New Patriotic Party (NPP) seeks to address the concern about extra fees in public schools, but its impact is unclear.

10. N. Assié-Lumumba, "Empowerment of Women in Higher Education in Africa: The Role and Mission of Research," UNESCO Forum on Education, Research and Knowledge, Occasional Paper no. 11, UNESCO, Paris, June 2006, http://unesdoc.unesco.org/images/0015/001510/151051eo.pdf.

11. H. Alderman and E. M. King, "Gender Differences in Parental Investment in Education," *Structural Change and Economic Dynamics* 9, no. 4 (1998): 453–468.

12. A. Stambach, *Lessons from Mount Kilimanjaro: Schooling, Community, and Gender in East Africa* (New York: Routledge, 2000).

13. See E. Cooke, S. Hague, and A. McKay, "The Ghana Poverty and Inequality Report," UNICEF, 2016, https://www.unicef.org/ghana/Ghana_Poverty_and_Inequality_Analysis_FINAL_Match_2016(1).pdf. Cooke, Hague, and McKay note: "Ghana uses two poverty lines; an upper one below which an individual is considered to be unable to meet all their food and non-food needs, and a lower poverty line below which an individual is considered unable to even meet their food needs. The upper poverty line is set at 1,314 GHS per adult per year for 2013, and households below it are simply referred to throughout this paper as living in poverty. The lower poverty line is set at 792 GHS per adult per year, and households below it are referred to throughout as living in extreme poverty." Quotation on p. 5.

14. The following specific actions were implemented. The school:
    - Admitted more girls.
    - Posted motivational sayings across the classrooms, hallways, and bulletins.
    - Affirmed courageous decisions, such as encouraging sexual-harassment reporting by ensuring anonymity and taking actions toward the accused.
    - Created girls' clubs and hosted Sunday talks focused on feminine hygiene and leadership.
    - Emphasized self-discipline through incentives that rewarded punctuality.
    - Centered faith-based learning through morning prayer.
    - Changed policies that favored boys, such as only allowing males to give speeches.

15. G. J. S. Dei, "Learning Culture, Spirituality and Local Knowledge: Implications for African Schooling," *International Review of Education* 48, no. 5 (2002): 335–360.

16. United Nations Educational, Scientific and Cultural Organization, "Girls Education—The Facts," Fact Sheet, Education for All Global Moni-

toring Report, UNESCO, October 2013, http://en.unesco.org/gem-report /sites/gem-report/files/girls-factsheet-en.pdf.

4. The Limits of Confidence and the Problem with Achievement

1. See, for example, "How Schools Shortchange Girls: The AAUW Report," commissioned by the AAUW Educational Foundation, researched by the Wellesley College Center for Research on Women, American Association of University Women, 1992. Parts of the report available at https://history.aauw.org/aauw-research/1992-how-schools -shortchange-girls. Also published as *How Schools Shortchange Girls: The AAUW Report* (New York: Marlowe, 1995); A. L. Duckworth and M. E. Seligman, "Self-Discipline Gives Girls the Edge: Gender in Self-Discipline, Grades, and Achievement Test Scores," *Journal of Educational Psychology* 98, no. 1 (2006): 198–208; K. Kay and C. Shipman, "The Confidence Gap," *Atlantic*, May 2014, 1–18.

2. "How Schools Shortchange Girls," 3.

3. "How Schools Shortchange Girls," 19.

4. "How Schools Shortchange Girls," 9.

5. "How Schools Shortchange Girls," 9.

6. "How Schools Shortchange Girls," 47–48.

7. P. Orenstein, *Schoolgirls: Young Women, Self-Esteem, and the Confidence Gap* (New York: Doubleday, 1994). See also M. Sadker and D. Sadker, *Failing at Fairness: How America's Schools Cheat Girls* (New York: Charles Scribner's Sons, 1994).

8. "How Schools Shortchange Girls," 19–21.

9. See, for example, T. R. Buckley and R. T. Carter, "Black Adolescent Girls: Do Gender Role and Racial Identity Impact Their Self-Esteem?" *Sex Roles* 53, no. 9 (2005): 647–661.

10. C. Riegle-Crumb, C. Moore, and A. Ramos-Wada, "Who Wants to Have a Career in Science or Math? Exploring Adolescents' Future Aspirations by Gender and Race/Ethnicity," *Science Education* 95, no. 3 (2011):

458–476. The same applies to the achievement levels of Black and Hispanic males in math and science.

11. "How Schools Shortchange Girls." See also R. Epstein, J. Blake, and T. González, "Girlhood Interrupted: The Erasure of Black Girls' Childhood," Center on Poverty and Inequality, Georgetown Law, Washington DC, 2017, https://www.law.georgetown.edu/poverty-inequality -center/wp-content/uploads/sites/14/2017/08/girlhood-interrupted.pdf.

12. K. O. Asante, "Sex Differences in Mathematics Performance among Senior High Students in Ghana," *Gender and Behaviour* 8, no. 2 (2010): 3279–3289.

13. J. I. Nyala, "Sex-Differences in Attitude towards Mathematics of Junior High School Students in Ghana," *Edo Journal of Counselling* 1, no. 1 (2008): 137–161.

14. E. Ampadu, "Beliefs, Attitudes and Self-Confidence in Learning Mathematics among Basic School Students in the Central Region of Ghana," *Mathematics Connection* 8, no. 1 (2009): 45–56; L. Kyei, B. Apam, and K. S. Nokoe, "Some Gender Differences in Performance in Senior High Mathematics Examinations in Mixed High Schools," *American Journal of Social and Management Science* 2, no. 4 (2011): 348–355.

15. G. K. Agbley, "'My Brother Says Girls Don't Do Mathematics': Girls' Educational Experiences and Secondary School Programme Choices in Ghana," *UDS International Journal of Development* 2, no. 1 (2015): 206–221.

16. Kay and Shipman, "Confidence Gap."

17. See J. Ehrlinger and D. Dunning, "How Chronic Self-Views Influence (and Potentially Mislead) Estimates of Performance," *Journal of Personality and Social Psychology*, 84, no. 1 (2003): 5–17; E. Reuben, P. Rey-Biel, P. Sapienza, and L. Zingales, "The Emergence of Male Leadership in Competitive Environments," *Journal of Economic Behavior and Organization* 83, no. 1 (June 2012): 111–117.

18. Kay and Shipman, "Confidence Gap." See also C. Anderson, S. Brion, D. A. Moore, and J. A. Kennedy, "A Status-Enhancement Account of

Overconfidence," *Journal of Personality and Social Psychology* 103, no. 4 (2012): 718–735.

19. G. E. Miller, T. Yu, E. Chen, and G. H. Brody, "Self-Control Forecasts Better Psychosocial Outcomes but Faster Epigenetic Aging in Low-SES Youth." *Proceedings of the National Academy of Sciences* 112, no. 33 (2015): 10325–10330.

20. The only year in which Ghana, South Africa, and the United States participated in TIMSS was 2011. The best data was available for eighth-grade math scores. Unless otherwise noted, each figure included in this chapter represents eighth-grade math scores.

21. In the analysis on Ghana, I do not make a distinction regarding race, as over 90 percent of the population is Black.

22. TIMSS has a two-stage design in which schools are sampled in the first stage, and then two classrooms are sampled from within each of the selected schools in the second stage.

23. Responses to questions are analyzed by socioeconomic characteristics at the individual and school/neighborhood level in addition to race and gender. Parental education and income, as well as the percentage of the school's students that is affluent versus economically disadvantaged, is also considered. These factors are examined in relation to self-concept questions and how they impact the average score in math and science, which was determined by TIMSS with the use of item response theory. Multivariate regressions were conducted for statistical significance. Students' responses are gauged based on how much they agree with the following statements:
    - "I enjoy learning science (or math)." (Enjoyment of subject)
    - "I believe I can do well in science (or math)." (Confidence)
    - "Learning science (or math) is useful for me and/or my future career." (Value)

24. Coincidentally, the number of private schools in Ghana increased by 36 percent between 2005 and 2008 (C. Sakellariou, "Decomposing the Increase in TIMSS Scores in Ghana: 2003–2007," Policy Working Research Paper no. 6084, Human Development Network Education Unit,

World Bank, June 2012, http://documents.worldbank.org/curated/en /705881468031495601/pdf/WPS6084.pdf), so it may be that these improvements occurred with the advent of private schools. However, even if true, the link is unproven.

25. See G. Frempong, M. Visser, N. Feza, L. Winnaar, and S. Nuamah, "Resilient Learners in Schools Serving Poor Communities," *Electronic Journal of Research in Educational Psychology* 14, no. 2 (2016): 352–367.

26. A. Ginsburg, G. Cooke, S. Leinwand, J. Noell, and E. Pollock, "Reassessing US International Mathematics Performance: New Findings from the 2003 TIMSS and PISA," American Institutes for Research, Washington, DC, November 2005, www.cimm.ucr.ac.cr/ojs/index.php /eudoxus/article/viewFile/446/445.

27. J. S. Hyde and J. E. Mertz, "Gender, Culture, and Mathematics Performance," *Proceedings of the National Academy of Sciences* 106, no. 22 (2009): 8801–8807.

28. See, for example, L. Guiso, F. Monte, P. Sapienza, and L. Zingales, "Culture, Gender, and Math," *Science* 320, no. 5880 (2008): 1164–1165.

29. According to the data in 2011, in eighth grade, Black girls and boys who attend a school in which more than 50 percent of the students are disadvantaged have an average math score of 454, while Hispanics have an average score of 472, Whites an average score of 512, and Asians an average score of 534. Altogether, disadvantaged Black students score 18 points lower than Hispanics, 66 points lower than Whites, and 80 points lower than Asians. In other words, Black boys and girls clearly have the lowest math scores.

30. For this group, there was a 24 percent increase in students scoring above 400, up from 10 percent to 34 percent.

31. G. Frempong, "Equity and Quality Mathematics Education within Schools: Findings from TIMSS Data for Ghana," *African Journal of Research in Mathematics, Science and Technology Education* 14, no. 3 (2010): 50–62.

32. J. Seekings and N. Nattrass, *Class, Race, and Inequality in South Africa* (New Haven: Yale University Press, 2008).

33. S. F. Reardon, E. M. Fahle, D. Kalogrides, A. Podolsky, and R. C. Zarate, "Gender Achievement Gaps in US School Districts," CEPA Working Paper No. 18-13, Center for Education Policy Analysis, Stanford University, June 2018, https://cepa.stanford.edu/sites/default/files /wp18-13-v201806_0.pdf.

34. Miller, Yu, Chen, and Brody, "Self-Control Forecasts Better Psychosocial Outcomes."

Conclusion

1. Plan International, "The State of Gender Equality for US Adolescents: Full Research Findings from a National Survey of Adolescents," Perry Undem Research / Communication, September 12, 2018, https://www .planusa.org/docs/state-of-gender-equality-2018.pdf.

2. A. Onyeka-Crawford, K. Patrick, and N. Chaudhry, "Let Her Learn: Stopping School Pushout for Girls of Color," National Women's Law Center, 2017, https://nwlc.org/wp-content/uploads/2017/04/final_nwlc _Gates_GirlsofColor.pdf.

3. "Ghanaians Fume as Otiko Tells Girls Not to Attract Rapists with Short Skirts," Citi 97.3 FM, Citi Newsroom, March 26, 2017, http:// citifmonline.com/2017/03/26/social-media-fumes-as-otiko-tells-girls -no-to-attract-rapists-with-short-skirts/.

4. Women's March, "The March," 2017, https://www.womensmarch.com /march/.

5. According to Myra Ferree, a women's movement has to do with the constituency that is organizing as an interest group but does not imply that the actions they are taking are connected to gender, thus "many mobilizations of women as women start out with a non-gender-directed goal, such as peace . . . and only later develop an interest in changing gender relations . . . Activism for the purpose of changing women's subordination to men is what defines 'feminism.'" See M. Ferree, "Globalization and Feminism," *Global Feminism: Transnational Women's Activism, Organizing, and Human Rights,* ed. M. M. Ferree and A. M. Tripp. New York: NYU Press, 2006, quotation on p. 6.

6. A. M. Tripp, "Challenges in Transnational Feminist Mobilization," in Ferree and Tripp, eds., *Global Feminism*.

7. M. V. Harris-Perry, *Sister Citizen: Shame, Stereotypes, and Black Women in America* (New Haven, CT: Yale University Press, 2011).

8. S. A. Nuamah, "Achievement Oriented: Developing Positive Academic Identities for Girl Students at an Urban School," *American Educational Research Journal*, June 2018, doi: 0002831218782670.

9. S. A. Nuamah, "Closing the Gap, Widening the Net," Chicago United, CID Talks, 2013, https://www.chicago-united.org/mpage/CIDTalksLibrary.

Resources

MANY RESOURCES ARE available to educators who wish to assess and address equity and safety in their schools. I have selected a sample of those most recent, accessible, and useful, and included my own assessment for those building feminist schools.

Feminist School Tool Kit

Is your school a gender-equitable institution? Assess your school's policies and practices using this checklist. If you find that you are saying "no" to some of these, then your school may be engaging in biased gender practices. Work with your students to become a feminist school!

Physical Environment

- Does your school have flush toilets?
- Are there separate bathroom facilities, and are they open to students based on their preferred gender identification?
- Are there gender-neutral bathrooms?
- Do you provide free sanitary pads?
- Does your school maintain its supplies of toilet paper?

Classroom Instruction

- Do you ask students what pronoun they identify with?
- Do your textbook examples defy gender-based stereotypes?
- Are girls and boys grouped together on projects?
- During gym or dance class are gender-neutral roles promoted?
- Do you ensure that girls and boys are participating in class at similar levels?
- Do you openly talk about menstruation *and* puberty in sex-education courses?
- Do you teach students to recognize abuse and give them the resources to respond?

School Policies

- Is there a specific place for students to report sexual abuse or misconduct?
- Are students reprimanded for reporting what happened to them?
- Are girls and boys able to wear the school uniform option that is most comfortable to them?
- Are girls and boys held to the same standard in terms of their body language?
- Do your curricula and policies account for those who may be differently abled, trans, queer, or gender-fluid?

Research and Data

- Do you ask students about their needs annually?
- Do you make this data available to all stakeholders— parents, teachers, community partners?
- Do you regularly assess your policies and design interventions to respond to them?

Let's continue to build this assessment together. Send your ideas to howgirlsachieve@gmail.com.

Tool Kits for Building Safe and Equitable Schools

Advocating for Change for Adolescents! A Practical Toolkit for Young People to Advocate for Improved Adolescent Health and Well-Being. Women Deliver: The Partnership for Maternal, Newborn, and Child Health, May 2017, http://www.who.int /pmnch/knowledge/publications/advocacy_toolkit.pdf?ua=1

Bever, S. *Creating Supportive Learning Environments for Girls and Boys: A Guide for Educators.* IREX, n.d., https://www.irex.org /resource/creating-supportive-learning-environments-girls -and-boys-guide-educators

Let Her Learn: A Tool Kit to Stop School Pushout for Girls of Color. Washington, DC: National Women's Law Center, n.d., https:// nwlc.org/wp-content/uploads/2016/11/final_nwlc_NOVO2016 Toolkit.pdf

Morris, M. W., R. Epstein, and A. Yusuf. *Be Her Resource: A Toolkit about School Resource Officers and Girls of Color.* Washington, DC: National Black Women's Justice Institute and the Georgetown Law Center on Poverty and Inequality, https://www.law.georgetown.edu/poverty-inequality-center /wp-content/uploads/sites/14/2018/05/17_SRO-final-_Acc .pdf

Smith, J., M. Huppuch, M. Van Deven, and Girls for Gender Equity. *Hey! Shorty: A Guide to Combating Sexual Violence and Harassment in Schools and on the Streets.* New York: Feminist Press, 2011.

Watson, D., J. Hagopian, and W. Au. *Teaching for Black Lives.* Milwaukee, WI: Rethinking Schools, 2018. Available at:

https://www.rethinkingschools.org. This book contains valuable writing exercises similar to those that follow here.

"Womanist Women" Letter Writing Activity

Today, students are as exposed to issues across the globe as their parents. Thus, schools are increasingly forced to help students process the news around them rather than ignore it. One such issue includes the increasing public awareness of unarmed black adults and youth killed by police. African Americans, specifically, respond to these public incidents by reporting more stress, trauma, and overall lower mental well-being (see Jacob Bor et al., "Police Killings and Their Spillover Effects on the Mental Health of Black Americans," *Lancet* 392, 10144 [2018]: 302–310). Feminist schools, therefore, have a responsibility to help students contend with these negative experiences. This can be accomplished in many ways. Teele Elementary, the school featured in Chapter 2, encourages students to write letters to the victims of the police shootings. The letters help young people feel that they are taking action toward the issue of police violence. Writing activities cultivate empathy and provide an outlet for students to express how they feel. Below are samples of two writing projects from girl students at Teele Elementary. Try this type of activity with your students as well.

Letters to the Deceased

> Dear Freddie Gray,
>
> Your story impact my life because you were too young to die and it opened my eyes to see that black people are treated like this. And you also impact my life by making me notice that black people should be treated with respect and fairness. Last thing I want to say is don't re-

gret being black. Love your race and be proud of who
you are. Love,

Dear Tamir Rice,

I know this letter will never reach you but I wanted to
say this was really unfair. It was just a toy or nerf gun or
a watergun. You did not do anything wrong, innocent!
And the police did not get charged. This means a lot to
me because I have 12 toy guns and me and my friends
play with them every day. Let god bless you and I hope
you made it heaven.

Dear Kendra James,

You inspire me but you wasn't armed and you should not
get arrested and a police officer fired by self-defense by
struggling with James and you is so innocent to other
people and you got shot in the head and got pulled over.
And he arrested when he is in the driver seat. James was
shot in the head by a police officer in Portland, Oregon.
On May 5th, 2003 after the car in which she was a pas-
senger was pulled over. I am sorry for your incident.

Dear Rekia Boyd,

If you were alive, I'd wish you were my best friend. Your
story was inspiring but sad. It makes me want to stick
up for people who has gotten that done to them. You
knew you couldn't do much but you were strong. As
strong as you can be. You are strong, powerful and brave.
I'm sorry your killer wasn't arrested, what a shame it is.
But even though you died our strong. You're still strong
and you will always be strong. #BLACKLIVES MATTER
Sincerely,
BLACKS LOVE YOU.

Dear Tamir Rice,

I agree that 12 is still a kid and WHO WOULD KILL A KID? It just feels bad not to live a long life. So, I am here to say there is good news, people are protesting and trying to stand up or the people who were shot or no reason. Now you won't have to feel bad. People care for you as a black so be proud that you have brothers and sisters standing up for you.
GOD BLESS YOU.

Girls Speak
What impact does Black Lives Matter have on your future?

I will not tolerate anyone being racist to another person in front of me because the racist problem will gain more throughout the world and then people of color will feel un-belonging and sad and they don't matter. So, in the future everyone should know that their special in many ways!

I can walk outside my outside and not see a black person being searched or arrested or in fight because [they] created the black lives matter movement to help black people become the same as white people. They wanted to make, not just an equal community but an equal world. So now every time I walk out my house, I smile, because nothing bad is happening and I know why.

Because of the Black lives matter movement things are going a lot smoother than before and now with time to save others the movement and make it even better so there won't be any racial profiling and everybody will get treated equally and the same and no one will raise the question: what race are you?

In the future blacks are going to be treated more fairly.

Because being a black girl of color, my opinions won't always matter. even though no one is the same, I am still human, god just made me this way.

Being a young, Black woman, I might not be who people want me to be but this movement show no matter how much hate I get because of my skin color, I know that I matter so that's all that matter. Even I may be different from the world I know that these women gave me the right to speak my mind and I matter and so do you.

Why are women's rights important to you?

Dear Girls and Women,
You are not perfect but brilliant. You matter. You have
    something to say. You are smart. You are lucky to be
    a girl. You are brave and smart. You are beautiful.
I am brave, I am smart. I love myself. A woman's work
    is very hard.
I am myself . . . and that is how a woman is.

63 million girls can't go to school.
1 out of 3 women can't read
Only 10 percent of government is female.
Girls are supposed to learn.
Girls are intelligent and matter.
Girls can work wherever they want.
Girls are incredible.
The end.

Further Reading

Adichie, C. N. 2014. *We Should All Be Feminists*. New York: Vintage.

——. 2017. *Dear Ijeawele, or A Feminist Manifesto in Fifteen Suggestions*. New York: Knopf.

Albertyn, C. 2007. "Substantive Equality and Transformation in South Africa." *South African Journal on Human Rights* 23, no. 2: 253–276.

Alexander, K., D. Entwisle, and L. Olson. 2014. *The Long Shadow: Family Background, Disadvantaged Urban Youth, and the Transition to Adulthood*. New York: Russell Sage Foundation.

Anzaldúa, G. 1987. *Borderlands: la frontera* (vol. 3). San Francisco: Aunt Lute.

Bourdieu, P. and J. C. Passeron. 1977. *Reproduction in Education, Society, and Culture*. London: Sage.

Butler, J. 1990. *Gender Trouble and the Subversion of Identity*. New York: Routledge.

Carter, Prudence. 2005. *Keepin' It Real: School Success Beyond Black and White*. New York: Oxford University Press.

Cooper, B. C. 2017. *Beyond Respectability: The Intellectual Thought of Race Women*. Carbondale: University of Illinois Press.

Cooper, B. C., S. M. Morris, and R. M. Boylorn. 2017. *The Crunk Feminist Collection*. Old Westbury, NY: Feminist Press.

Cox, A. M. 2015. *Shapeshifters: Black Girls and the Choreography of Citizenship*. Durham, NC: Duke University Press.

Davis, A. Y. 2011. *Women, Race, & Class*. New York: Vintage.

Dosekun, S. 2007. "Defending Feminism in Africa." *postamble* 3, no. 1: 41–47.

Duckworth, A. L., C. Peterson, M. D. Matthews, and D. R. Kelly. 2007. "Grit: Perseverance and Passion for Long-Term Goals." *Journal of Personality and Social Psychology* 92, no. 6: 1087–1101.

Dumais, S. A. 2002. "Cultural Capital, Gender, and School Success: The Role of Habitus." *Sociology of Education* 75, no. 1: 44–68.

Farrington, C. A., M. Roderick, E. Allensworth, J. Nagaoka, T. S. Keyes, D. W. Johnson, and N. O. Beechum. 2012. *Teaching Adolescents to Become Learners: The Role of Non-cognitive Factors in Shaping School Performance—A Critical Literature Review*. Chicago: Consortium on Chicago School Research.

Freire, P. 1973. *Education for Critical Consciousness*. New York: Bloomsbury.

González, L. 1988. "For an Afro–Latin American Feminism." Pages 95–101 in *Women Organizing for Change: Confronting the Crisis in Latin America*. Isis International and DAWN.

Gunderson, E. A., G. Ramirez, S. C. Levine, and S. L. Beilock. 2012. "The Role of Parents and Teachers in the Development of Gender-Related Math Attitudes." *Sex Roles* 66, no. 3–4: 153–166.

Hess, D. E., and P. McAvoy. 2014. *The Political Classroom: Evidence and Ethics in Democratic Education*. New York: Routledge.

hooks, b. 2000. *Feminism Is for Everybody: Passionate Politics*. Boston: South End Press.

Hudson-Weems, C. 1994. *Africana Womanism: Reclaiming Ourselves*. Boston: Bedford Publishing.

Hull, Gloria, P. Bell, and B. Smith. "All the Women Are White and All the Blacks Are Men." *But Some of Us Are Brave: Black Women's Studies* (Old Westbury, NY: Feminist Press, 1982.

Kochiyama, Y., and K. Aguilar-San Juan. 1997. *Dragon Ladies: Asian American Feminists Breathe Fire.* Boston: South End Press.

Lopez, N. 2003. *Hopeful Girls, Troubled Boys: Race and Gender Disparity in Urban Education.* New York: Routledge.

Lorde, A. 1984. "Age, Race, Class, and Sex: Women Redefining Difference." Pages 114–123 in *Sister Outsider: Essays and Speeches.* Berkeley, CA: Crossing Press.

———1984. "The Master's Tools Will Never Dismantle the Master's House." Pages 110–113 in *Sister Outsider: Essays and Speeches.* Berkeley, CA: Crossing Press.

———1984. *Sister Outsider: Essays and Speeches.* Berkeley, CA: Crossing Press.

Mansbridge, J. 1993. "Feminism and Democratic Community." *Nomos* 35: 339–395.

McKenzie, M. 2014. *Black Girl Dangerous: On Race, Queerness, Class and Gender.* Oakland, CA: BGD Press.

Mikell, G. 1995. "African Feminism: Toward a New Politics of Representation." *Feminist Studies* 21, no. 2: 405–424.

Mikell, G., ed. 1997. *African Feminism: The Politics of Survival in Sub-Saharan Africa.* Philadelphia: University of Pennsylvania Press.

Mohanty, C. T. 1988. "Under Western Eyes: Feminist Scholarship and Colonial Discourses." *Feminist Review* 30: 61–88.

Moraga, C., and G. Anzaldúa, eds. 2015. *This Bridge Called My Back: Writings by Radical Women of Color*, 4th ed. Albany, NY: SUNY Press.

Ogbu, J. 1985. "Cultural Ecology of Competence among Inner-City Blacks." *In Black Children's Social, Educational, and Parent Environments*, edited by H. McAdoo and J. McAdoo. Newbury Park, CA: Sage.

Ransby, B. 2003. *Ella Baker and the Black Freedom Movement: A Radical Democratic Vision.* Chapel Hill, NC: University of North Carolina Press.

———2012. *Arrested Justice: Black Women, Violence, and America's Prison Nation.* New York: New York University Press.

Ritchie, A., C. B. Lloyd, and M. Grant. 2004. "Gender Differences in Time Use among Adolescents in Developing Countries: Implications of Rising School Enrollment Rates." Policy Research Division Working Paper, 193. New York: Population Council. http://www.popcouncil.org/pdfs/wp/193.pdf.

Roberts, D. E. 1999. *Killing the Black Body: Race, Reproduction, and the Meaning of Liberty.* New York: Vintage Books.

Shange, N. 1975. *For Colored Girls Who Have Considered Suicide / When the Rainbow Is Enuf.* Reprint ed.: New York: Simon and Schuster, 2010.

Smail, B. 1984. *Girl-Friendly Science: Avoiding Sex Bias in the Curriculum. Developing the Curriculum for a Changing World.* Schools Council Programme 3. York: Longman.

Smith, B., ed. 1983. *Home Girls: A Black Feminist Anthology.* Brunswick, NJ: Rutgers University Press.

Spivak, G. C. 1990. "'Can the Subaltern Speak?' Revised Edition, from the 'History' Chapter of *Critique of Postcolonial Reason.*" Pages 21–78 in *Can the Subaltern Speak? Reflections on the History of an Idea,* ed. R. C. Morris. New York: Columbia University Press.

Twist, L., and M. Sainsbury. 2009. "Girl Friendly? Investigating the Gender Gap in National Reading Tests at Age 11." *Educational Research* 51, no. 2: 283–297.

Walton, G. M., and G. L. Cohen. 2007. "A Question of Belonging: Race, Social Fit, and Achievement." *Journal of Personality and Social Psychology* 92, no. 1: 82.

Warikoo, N. 2005. "Gender and Ethnic Identity among Second-Generation Indo-Caribbeans." *Ethnic and Racial Studies* 28, no. 5: 803–831.

Acknowledgments

I didn't know it at the time, but I started writing this book on a plane ride in December 2016 from Accra, Ghana, where I had spent some time with three girls I had been working with since 2009. Our time together, as always, left me in awe. My goal was simply to write a short journal entry about it, but I ended up writing for eight hours. So, first, I want to thank those three girls. All the content for this book has been conceived over the course of knowing them. They let me into their lives and taught me so much not only about gender, education, and public policy but also about empathy, humility, and especially faith in God. They have made me a better scholar, friend, daughter, and person. I am forever grateful for our friendship.

Before this book was a book, it was an idea that my time at the Women and Public Policy Program at the Harvard Kennedy School allowed me to flesh out. I presented an initial chapter at a seminar in January 2017, and it was their generous feedback and positive reception that made me believe it was something I could develop into a potential book manuscript. Special thanks to my mentor there, Iris Bohnet, academic dean and co-director of the Women and Public Policy Program, for our many conversations in her office, and especially to Nicole Carter Quinn, the director of research and operations of the program at the time, for her specific advice and continued help as I began to navigate the process.

At this point I must thank Thomas LeBien, executive editor-at-large at Harvard University Press, who believed in the project very early on and continued to be invested, even as it radically transformed. I am deeply appreciative of his accessibility, which was critical to this first-time author, and the lengths he took to be an advocate for this project in unprecedented ways. He made the process of writing an exciting one. A huge thanks to the entire Harvard University Press team!

On a related note, special thanks to Amy Reeve, who talked with me and edited earlier rough versions of the manuscript. Her serious engagement with my ideas helped convince me the book was a real thing. Thank you also to Jessica Hinds-Bond, who also helped to pull the manuscript together before and after the tremendously helpful feedback I received from anonymous reviewers.

Portions of Chapter 3 were first published online on June 28, 2018, as "Achievement Oriented: Developing Positive Academic Identities for Girl Students at an Urban School," in *American Educational Research Journal*. They are reprinted here with permission of Sage Publishing.

I thank my friends Kevin Levay, Oreoluwa Badaki, and many others who at some point read work related to this project. Similarly, I thank many colleagues and mentors at the University of Pennsylvania, Harvard University, and Princeton University, whom I admire and have the privilege of knowing. This list is long but especially includes Sigal Ben Porath, Traci Burch, Dan Gillion, Jane Mansbridge, Reuel Rogers, and Cecile Rouse. They each, at some point, encouraged me to move forward with the book when I felt stuck or feared that it was not the right time. I also want to thank my longtime mentor from the George Washington University, Professor Steve Balla, for his unrelenting support throughout my career.

I want to thank my dad for checking in on me during the writing stages. And a very special thanks to my amazing partner, Zeke, who helped me cross the finish line. For the past year and a half, at any given point he has acted as my chapter reader, spiritual counselor, part-time editor, full-time chef, and just all-around source of support. He joined me on my trip to South Africa, when I decided that I needed to return to collect more data right before the manuscript was due. While pursuing his own research, he somehow managed to help me story-board arguments on white boards and flash cards and even made them into fun games. He cooked meals, made tea, prayed, and just did whatever else I needed as I stayed up all hours of the night thinking through ideas. His help during the development of this book was invaluable.

Finally, I want to thank my closest friends on the planet: my mom, Afua Serwaah, and my brother, Robert Nuamah. The unconditional love and support that I have received from them since Day One is unmatched. I am especially grateful for our daily three-way phone calls, during which my mother reminds me that "I got it," or my brother exclaims, "you the best, Sal." It makes me feel as if nothing anyone else says matters. I thank God for their love; it's like a shield that protects me every day.

Routinely, my work reminds me that so many kids never get the chance to experience this type of love. Through my work, I am striving to share this love with others. This book is a small offering. So, thank you for reading it.

Index